GET FIRE'D UP

Build Wealth, Escape the 9-5 Trap, and Live Life on Your Terms

Omolola Oyewumi

Published by:
SBA Publishing
booksbysba@gmail.com
Ilupeju, Lagos
+234 813 647 4117
+234 815 271 8921

ACKNOWLEDGEMENT

Writing this book has been one of the most stretching, faith-deepening, and transformative journeys of my life. There were moments when the words came easily and moments when I had to dig deep, lean on grace, and remember why I started. I could never have done this alone, and I am truly grateful for the remarkable people who lifted, supported, and believed in me along the way.

To my mentor, friend, and pro-coach, **Debola Deji-Kurunmi (DDK)**, thank you for believing in my calling even before I fully understood the magnitude of it. When I entered the VCAP program, one of my goals was to write one book. You looked at that goal and, with your prophetic clarity, declared that I would not just write one, I would birth three. And that is exactly what happened.

Under your coaching, my vision expanded, my faith stretched, and my capacity grew. Today, I have written three books, published two this year, and I am preparing to release the third in the coming months. Thank you for sharpening my voice, strengthening my courage, and walking with me as this assignment unfolded. I honor you deeply.

To Dr. Oleg Konovalov, thank you for stretching my thinking through the Visionary Leadership program and helping me see myself not just as a wealth coach or author, but as a global Wealth Empowerment Voice for Professionals with influence beyond borders. Your strategic insight, challenging questions, and ability to unlock higher-level vision brought depth, structure, and a new dimension to this work. I am grateful for the way you helped me rise into the leader I am becoming.

To my Coach, **Seye Benjamin-Agbo,** and her incredible team at **SBA Publishing**, thank you for your excellence, patience, and unwavering commitment to bringing this book to life. Your professionalism and dedication to quality made this journey seamless. You handled my words with honor and stewarded this project as though it were your own. I am truly grateful.

To **Lady Bodam**, my support coach at VCAP, your wisdom, warmth, and structure have shaped me more than you know. Thank you for holding space for me to grow. To my support visionaries, **Bunmi Olugbeja** and **Ebunoluwa Opelami**, your gentle nudges, check-ins, and prayers kept me centered and consistent. You helped me stay anchored when the work felt heavy.

To my sisters by destiny, 'Mo Makanjuola and Perla Kolunga, Dr Bukola Adesanmi, Jade Fakoya, Dr Ibukunoluwa Ajayi-

Banji, and Christina Carter, thank you for cheering me on, praying with me, listening to me, and standing with me through every draft, every breakthrough, and every late-night moment of clarity and planning.

To my business partners at TeamIgnite, Strategic Team, and TeamPassionate, my mentor, Dr. Grace, Ms. Oge, Ms. Sola, Ms. Bennie, Ms. Vivian, Mr. Olalekan, thank you for believing in this mission and for journeying with me as we empower professionals and families to rewrite their financial stories.

To the Legacy Wealth Ladies, your encouragement, feedback, and steadfast support pushed me forward more times than you know. Thank you for keeping me accountable and inspired.

To my friends, family, and every single person who watched the kids, sent a prayer, checked in, or freed my hands so I could focus, research, record, and pour my heart into these pages—your sacrifice is part of this book. God sees it, and I honor you deeply.

And finally, to everyone whose name may not be written here but whose fingerprints are woven into this journey—thank you. Your support, kindness, and belief helped birth this masterpiece.

I appreciate you all more than words can express.

You are FIRE'D UP.

DEDICATION

To **God**, my eternal Source, thank you.

For years, I wanted to write this book. I started, paused, restarted, and waited for the right clarity and strength. This year, by Your grace and divine help, I finally finished it. Thank You for giving me the wisdom, discipline, and courage to bring this vision to life. Every page carries Your breath, Your wisdom, and Your leading. Thank You for trusting me with this assignment.

To my family, **my husband, and our three beautiful children,** thank you for the love, patience, and laughter that fill our home. Thank you for the room you gave me to dream, think, write, rewrite, research, record, and create. You are my joy, my grounding, and the first circle God blessed me with. This journey was lighter because of you.

To **my parents, my siblings, and my in-laws,** thank you. Every encouraging word, every helping hand, every moment you carried the load so I could focus, none of it was unnoticed. You are my foundation and my greatest blessing.

And to every dreamer who feels the pull of destiny, who knows there is more ahead of you than behind you, to everyone who knows deep down that you were made for more, may this book be the spark that awakens your courage, strengthen your confidence, fuel your faith, remind you that your dreams are possible and that God truly designed you for greatness.

This is for you.

FOREWORD

by Loral Langemeier

ost people think retirement is something that happens at 65 if they are lucky. They grind for decades, trade their time for money, and pray their 401(k) doesn't tank right before they finally get to "enjoy life." That is not a retirement plan. That is a gamble. And it is a losing one.

Omolola Oyewumi did not wait. She did not hope. She did not cross her fingers and pray the system would work in her favor. She built a plan, executed it, and retired at 40. Not because she won the lottery or married rich, but because she refused to accept financial fragility as her reality.

Here is what most people do not understand: relying on one paycheck is the riskiest financial decision you can make. One layoff. One recession. One health crisis. And decades of "security" vanish overnight. Omolola figured this out early. She looked at her corporate job, the promotions, the stability, the benefits, and saw it for what it really was: a single point of failure.

So, she did what every millionaire I know has done: she built multiple income streams, took control of her cash flow, and put her money to work instead of working for money her entire life.

This is not a theory. Omolola is an immigrant woman who juggled motherhood, education, and a demanding career while building the wealth that bought her freedom by 40. She did not have a trust fund. She did not have insider connections. She had discipline, strategy, and the guts to play a different game than everyone around her.

And that is exactly why I'm writing this foreword. Because Omolola gets what I've been teaching for years: wealth is built through assets and cash flow, not paychecks and hope. She diversified her income. She automated her systems. She invested strategically. She protected her wealth. And she aligned every financial decision with the life she actually wanted to live, not the one society told her to accept.

The FIRE'D Up Accelerator System™ she teaches in this book is not complicated, but it requires something most people are not willing to give: action. You cannot build wealth by reading about it. You can't retire early by thinking positive thoughts. You have to make moves. Build income streams. Control your cash flow. Invest with intention.

Stack assets that generate money while you sleep.

If you are reading this and thinking, "Yeah, but I'm not like her" or "That won't work for me," stop. That's exactly the scarcity mindset that keeps people broke. Omolola proves that financial independence is not reserved for a lucky few. But it is available to anyone willing to challenge the old rules, build the right systems, and take responsibility for their financial future.

The old retirement model is dead. You don't have to wait until you are too old to enjoy your life to finally have freedom. You can design it now. Omolola did it. I have done it. And if you're ready to stop making excuses and start building real wealth, this book will show you exactly how.

Your move.

Loral Langemeier

Millionaire Maker and Author of The Millionaire Maker

TABLE OF CONTENTS

Part I
— The Foundation

Part II —
The FIRE'd Up Accelerator System™

PART I

— THE FOUNDATION

INTRODUCTION

I magine a life where retirement becomes a tangible reality in your 40s or 50s, not a distant dream tied to the age of 65. A life where financial freedom goes beyond accumulating wealth, empowering you to make choices with confidence, live with purpose, and define success on your own terms. This is more than a mere dream; it's a reality within your reach.

A few years ago, I stepped onto American soil, thousands of miles from home. I left behind my children, my comfort zone, and everything familiar, armed with nothing but faith, dreams, and determination. Pursuing a master's degree in computer information systems and security at Prairie View A&M University became more than an academic milestone; it marked the beginning of designing a life where retirement would be defined by intentional choices rather than age. I was determined never to wait until I was "old enough" to retire. I wanted to redefine what retirement meant, especially for professionals and women like me from diverse backgrounds, who often carried both ambition and responsibility in equal measure.

Soon after I moved to America, my children joined me, and my world shifted once again. I found myself navigating pregnancy, motherhood, rigorous academics, and life's relentless curveballs, all while adjusting to a new culture. There were moments when quitting seemed easier than continuing. The thought of taking a leave of absence from my program was incredibly tempting, and I wanted to throw in the towel multiple times. But by God's grace, I pressed on. Despite every challenge, I graduated from the College of Engineering with a 3.91 GPA. This is resilience in action, faith, and focused intention.

Yet, my journey didn't end with that degree; it was merely the beginning of new beginnings. By the age of 40, I had officially stepped away from corporate America, walking boldly into a chapter I had envisioned years prior. Through strategic planning, intentional saving, diversified income streams, and learning about investments, I took control of my timeline. Today, my mission is to empower professionals, women, and immigrants to break free from society's traditional retirement timeline and achieve financial independence far sooner than expected.

A Gallup survey said that nearly 7 in 10 professionals hope to retire before 60, yet most admit their savings won't sustain that goal. This book is designed to bridge that gap. I wrote this because I know firsthand that Financial Independence and Early Retirement (FIRE) are not privileges reserved for a select few. They are attainable milestones within your grasp. Consider this book your blueprint, your companion, and your empowerment toolkit, crafted to help you diversify your income, build generational wealth, and retire decades earlier than convention suggests.

Within these pages, you'll find principles, actionable steps, and real-life stories that made accelerated financial independence possible. By holding this guide, you're entering an awakening, a moment where you realize that early retirement can be mapped, planned, and achieved on your own terms.

The Decision That Changed Everything

My years in corporate sharpened my skills but often drained my spirit. The pivotal awakening came when I realized retirement doesn't have to be the end. It can be the beginning of freedom, creativity, family, impact, and legacy. When I made the bold decision to retire from corporate life at 40, it wasn't because I stumbled upon a secret formula; it was because I made four very intentional choices.

First, I accepted the truth that relying on a single paycheck is a form of financial fragility. The illusion of security that a monthly salary provides can be dangerous. It feels stable until it suddenly isn't. I realized that one employer's decision, one economic downturn, or even one health crisis could undo years of effort. That awakening shifted my perspective on income. I began building multiple income streams, both active and passive, that provided me options, security, and freedom of choice. I explored ways to monetize my knowledge, invest wisely, and create assets that could grow without my constant presence. Having multiple sources of income didn't just increase my earnings; it expanded my confidence. It meant that no single setback could derail my destiny.

Second, I took complete control of my cash flow. I stopped letting money slip through my hands unnoticed. I paid down debt, tracked every dollar, and built systems that kept me accountable. I learned that discipline is not restriction but empowerment. I created systems that reflected my priorities, automated my savings and investments, ensuring my money worked for me rather than against me.

Third, I embraced the power of investing and compounding. I stopped seeing investing as something reserved for the wealthy or the "financially savvy." Instead, I began to see it as an act of stewardship, putting my money to work with wisdom and purpose. Every dollar I invested became a seed, and like any seed, it needed time, care, and consistency to grow.

I became deliberate about protecting and expanding my wealth, ensuring every dollar was safeguarded, tax-optimized, and positioned for long-term growth. I educated myself about stocks, real estate, retirement accounts, and other vehicles that could multiply wealth over time.

Finally, I developed a vision-driven plan that aligned my money with my values, my faith, and the legacy I wanted to leave behind. Wealth is a tool. I wanted my financial decisions to reflect what mattered most: faith, family, and future impact. My plan wasn't just about early retirement; it was about freedom; freedom to serve, to give, to love, to live with intention, and to pass on a legacy that outlives me.

These decisions became the foundation of what I now call the FIRE'D UP Accelerator System™, which is the exact system that helped me break free from paycheck dependence and walk confidently into financial freedom. And it's the system I'll walk you through in this book.

What You'll Gain in This Book

At its heart, this book is an invitation to freedom, an opportunity to redefine how we view retirement and reclaim the power to live life on our own terms. Within these pages, you will see that financial independence and early retirement are not far-off dreams but real, attainable possibilities.

You won't just walk through my story; you'll trace a pattern that many others have followed to build extraordinary wealth, retire earlier than expected, and most importantly, live with intention. I didn't invent this path. I learned it through mentorship, coaching, study, and by observing ordinary professionals master their finances, grow their wealth, and align their financial decisions with their faith and values. Watching them succeed made me believe I could do it too. Doing it convinced me that you can as well.

In this book, we are redefining F.I.R.E. (Financial Independence, Retire Early). You don't have to wait until 65 to retire. You can design a life so fulfilling that you no longer need to escape from it. As you read, you'll uncover the scarcity beliefs that quietly sabotage your wealth and learn how to rewire them for abundance. You'll define what fulfillment truly means to you so that money becomes a servant to your purpose, not the other way around.

Then, we'll walk through the FIRE'D UP Accelerator System™ pillars you can start applying immediately:

- Income Diversification (Make Money): why relying on one paycheck is financial fragility, and how to build multiple active and passive income streams that secure your future and create freedom of choice.

- Money Mastery Systems (Manage Money): how to take control of your cash flow, wipe out debt, and automate your finances so your money grows on autopilot, giving you mastery instead of money stress.

- Wealth Growth & Protection (Multiply & Protect Money): how to invest, compound, and protect wealth strategically, so every dollar you grow is safeguarded, tax-optimized, and positioned for long-term financial independence.

- Life & Wealth Design (Money with Meaning): how to create a vision-driven wealth plan that aligns your money with your values, faith, freedom, and legacy, ensuring that FIRE goes beyond early retirement, anchoring it in a life filled with meaning.

You'll learn how immigrants like me turned restrictions into opportunities, how to transition gracefully from a 9-5 job into entrepreneurship, how to assess your FIRE readiness and immediately be empowered with a roadmap to achieve financial independence, and how to build trans-generational wealth that outlives you.

Beyond strategies and systems, you'll also find stories, reflection prompts, and actionable steps to help you put this into practice in your own life. You are invited to think bigger, act bolder, and see financial independence as something within your reach, no matter your background or starting point.

And finally, my joy would be for you to join the movement, the FIRE'D UP Collective. This is where your journey truly expands beyond these pages into a community of professionals worldwide who are redefining what retirement means in the twenty-first century.

Welcome to Get FIRE'D UP beyond the paycheck. Your journey starts here.

Chapter
One

1 RETIRED BEFORE 40 - YOU CAN TOO

"Retirement is not the finish line; it is the new beginning. Retirement is not your last paragraph; it is the long, rich, rewarding final chapters of your own book."

— *Chris Hogan*

The Retirement Lie We've Been Told

Growing up in Africa, the path to retirement seemed certain. Study hard, secure a respected profession, remain loyal to it for thirty-plus years, and if fortune smiles upon you, step away at 65 with a pension. That formula was presented as the honorable path, the one that guaranteed stability and respect. It was echoed by teachers, reinforced at family gatherings, and woven into our cultural narratives. However, what no one said out loud was that this same formula often led down a path full of limitations. It was a path that kept too many people waiting to live, even as life had already passed them by.

Even as a young girl, I found myself questioning it. Why must we wait until old age to live life fully? Why must we work so hard just to settle for the bare minimum? Why should dreams of freedom be postponed until the last chapter of life? Why should dreams of travel, fun legacy, or impact be delayed until our bodies are weary and our best years behind us? I didn't have the right words then, but I sensed deep inside that there had to be another way. A different script that allowed us to enjoy our most vibrant years, not just survive them. I didn't know it at the time, but my own journey through immigration, education, corporate America, motherhood, and mindset would lead me to challenge this outdated retirement paradigm and eventually shatter it.

Awakening to New Possibilities

When I came to America, I carried two suitcases: one visible, one invisible. The visible one held my belongings, clothes, documents, and essentials, while the invisible one carried legacy, vision, sacrifice, and relentless hope.

My journey in corporate America was marked by ambition and a deep desire to break down barriers. After working my way through various roles, I finally landed a coveted role as a Product Manager in my dream company, Microsoft. On paper, this is the kind of job others admire. But behind the scenes, the reality was far less glamorous. It involved long work hours, grueling commutes, plenty of office politics, delayed promotions without explanation, and projects that drained me so much that I felt exhausted and hollow.

The pivotal moment came one evening when I realized this lifestyle was draining me not just professionally, but personally. I was giving my best hours to a job that left me mentally and physically exhausted. The long days, the constant deadlines, the meetings, scrum of scrums, and projects, they were taking more from me than I had realized.

I noticed the cost in the most important parts of my life: time with my children. Moments I could never get back were slipping away—bedtimes missed, conversations lost, and memories I missed out on. It became clear that this was more than just fatigue; it was a slow erosion of joy, peace, and presence.

That night, I asked myself a life-changing question: Is this what I want for the next twenty years?

The answer was a resounding NO.

It was not a reaction born of frustration alone but of clarity. I knew that if I continued this path, I would be trading my most valuable years for stability and security that felt increasingly hollow. That realization marked the beginning of a shift, one that would eventually lead me to reimagine how I lived, worked, and built a future that aligned with my values.

How I Built My Exit Plan

I knew something had to change. Every morning, I woke up, commuted to an office, and gave my best hours to a paycheck that could disappear overnight. I looked successful on the outside, but inside, I felt the weight of fragility. If my paycheck stopped, everything would stop with it.

While the realization was unsettling, it ignited a fire within me that could not be extinguished.

With this new sobering realization, I began to educate myself about money, not just how to earn it, but how to grow it and put it to work in ways that could create long-term stability. I immersed myself in books, night after night of watching YouTube videos on how money works, devoured practical guides, and paid close attention to the advice of mentors who had successfully built wealth through disciplined strategies. I studied the mechanics of money, learning how to manage it and make it serve my goals.

I came to understand the importance of controlling cash flow, knowing where every dollar went, and making intentional choices about how to use it. I learned the compounding power of investments, seeing clearly how even small, consistent steps could grow into significant financial security over time. Then I discovered the necessity of building multiple streams of income rather than relying solely on a single paycheck to reduce risk and create options for the future.

Through this process, my mindset shifted. I no longer saw myself simply as an employee exchanging hours for a salary. I began to see myself as a woman capable of creating wealth deliberately and purposefully. Someone who could design financial freedom with intention, rather than waiting for it to happen.

I started small. I mean, really small, because I was in debt. My very first coaching gig barely paid enough to cover my utility bills, but it carried a value far beyond the paycheck itself; it represented something priceless: freedom. For the first time, I experienced what it meant to earn outside of the confines of a traditional salary, to see that my time and effort could create opportunities beyond the office. That small taste of autonomy shifted my perspective and gave me a new sense of possibility.

From there, I began exploring other avenues to diversify my income. I invested time and resources into real estate, learning how to generate returns beyond a single paycheck. I tested the waters by opening a brokerage account and started buying REITs (Real Estate Investment Trusts) as small as $50. I began to understand the principles of long-term growth and the importance of disciplined investing. I opened an online store, building a small business that allowed me to create and sell on Shopify and Amazon KDP.

I also became a licensed insurance agent, gaining another avenue for professional and financial growth.

In addition, I launched a coaching practice, sharing knowledge and strategies that could empower others while generating income for myself. I authored three books, creating another stream that allowed me to establish myself as a writer and thought leader. Each new venture was like a seed planted in different soil. Some took longer than the others before producing visible results. However, over time, those seeds multiplied into multiple streams of income that continue to grow and support me today.

The process taught me patience, consistency, and the value of building wealth deliberately, step by step, decision by decision. I also leaned heavily on masterminds, mentorship, and accountability. I sought out people who challenged me to think bigger, who taught me strategies to accelerate my growth, and who reminded me that discipline was the bridge between my goals and the results I achieved. One of my mentors gave me a piece of advice that I still carry: *"Do not buy your second car until you have bought your second home (rental)."*

That single principle grounded me when my income started to rise. The truth is, I was distracted initially as an entrepreneur, chasing shiny objects, but I quickly stayed true to my money rules. While others around me were upgrading their lifestyles, purchasing new cars, taking on bigger expenses, and increasing their monthly obligations,

I focused on upgrading my assets instead. I made strategic purchases, invested wisely, and remained disciplined in my financial decisions.

Then came a company-wide reorganization that became a defining moment. My position was affected, and I was given the opportunity to apply for other roles within the organization. On paper, I could have continued my career trajectory and maintained the status quo. But deep down, my desire had always been to retire at 40, and I knew the moment I had been preparing for had arrived.

For years, I had been methodical, saving, investing, building multiple streams of income, and creating a financial runway that would allow me to step away without risk. I had laid the groundwork, and now it was time to act. The re-org wasn't a setback but a setup. It was the nudge I needed to finally take the leap of faith.

Meanwhile, in the very month I turned 40, I retired from corporate. I walked away with clarity and confidence, knowing I had designed a structure that would sustain me beyond a traditional paycheck. It was a deliberate choice; freedom earned through planning, discipline, and consistent action. Hence, the beginning of a chapter filled with entrepreneurship, meaningful work, and the building of generational wealth. For the first time, I was fully in control of my time, my work, and my life, stepping into a chapter defined by purpose, opportunity, and intentional living. I had designed my finances, built my income streams, and created the runway that allowed me to say,

"This is it. This is the life I choose."

Designing "The Future You Want" on Your Own Timeline

When people hear my story, they often lean in and ask: "So what was the secret?" I always smile because the truth is less glamorous than people expect. There was no secret. No windfall. No magic lottery ticket. What was there instead were principles, though simple, that were very powerful and that I applied with discipline and courage over time. I'm building my way here one decision at a time. And that's the part that matters most, which is available to anyone willing to reimagine their timeline, break free from paycheck dependence, and take consistent action.

Research shows that 88% of millionaires have built their wealth independently. Most millionaires did not start with inheritance or overnight success; they built step by step, treating their financial journey with the same focus and discipline as a project. Their stories remind us that wealth grows from intention, persistence, and clear design, not by chance.

For decades, we have been conditioned to believe in a single, narrow model of life: work hard, stay loyal to a single career, and grind until you reach 65, at which point, if you're lucky, you might finally get to live on your own terms. That model is presented as safe, responsible, and respectable, but it comes with a steep cost. The truth is, the later you wait, the higher the price.

Every year spent in the traditional model comes at the expense of your health, your relationships, and your ability to pursue what matters most to you. Choosing to delay life until a distant retirement date is, in many ways, a gamble, one that costs far more than just money.

I stand as living proof that you do not have to wait. Retiring early is not about escaping responsibility; it's about stepping into life on your own terms, with energy, focus, and a sense of purpose. It means using your most vibrant years, the years when you have both strength and clarity to live intentionally, rather than postponing your dreams for a distant future.

Early retirement allows you to reclaim time and attention for the things that matter most. It is the freedom to spend unhurried mornings with your loved ones and significant other, to fully engage in the moments that make life meaningful. It is the ability to take that trip you have been dreaming about without needing permission or approval. It is about channeling your energy into projects, work, volunteering, or causes that align with your values and ignite your passion, rather than simply filling your days with obligations that drain you.

The bigger lesson is this: your retirement timeline is not set in stone. It is not determined by societal expectations, your employer, or even your past mistakes. It is yours to design, intentionally and deliberately. With planning, discipline, desire, and faith, you can create a path that allows you to live fully in the years when most people are still trading their time for paychecks. That realization changes everything. It turns retirement from an endpoint into a beginning, a new chapter defined by freedom, creativity, and purpose.

So don't ask "Is it possible?" Ask instead: "What do I want my life to look like, and when do I want to start living it?" Because the moment you make that decision, you step out of the script written for you and begin authoring your own.

Action Steps:

Start Your FIRE Journey Now

Your first step toward financial independence is not in the stock market or real estate, it begins in your mindset and with absolute clarity. Before you build wealth, you must know where you stand and where you want to go. This chapter shares my story, inviting you to begin designing your own.

Here are the first practical steps to get started:

- **Assess your current financial position.** Write down your income, expenses, debt, and savings. Don't gloss over the numbers; clarity is power.

- **Set your early retirement goal.** Don't just vaguely wish for freedom. Decide the age. Picture the lifestyle. Write it down where you can see it daily because what gets written gets real.

- **_Identify your motivators. Ask yourself:_** Why do I want financial independence? Family? Freedom? Legacy? Your "why" will fuel your discipline when the "how" feels hard.

- **_List your first streams of income._** Brainstorm at least three ways you could earn beyond your paycheck. This can be consulting, a side hustle, digital products, or investing. Prove to yourself that you can make money outside of a job using skills you already have.

- **_Create a money rule._** Decide on one personal principle that will govern your spending (e.g., "Every raise goes into investments," or "No second car until a second home"). Simple rules build lifelong discipline.

- **_Find accountability._** Share your FIRE goal with someone you trust. Share your target age and why it matters. Accountability is the bridge between intention and action.

Think of these as starter seeds; small, intentional steps that, over time, compound into extraordinary change.

Chapter Summary

Early retirement is achievable. It begins with the choices you make today. My retirement from corporate at 40 was the result of deliberate decisions, disciplined planning, and the willingness to take control of my future rather than wait for circumstances to dictate it.

Relying on a single paycheck is fragile. Life can change in an instant, and no title, promotion, or security can guarantee that stability. Financial independence, on the other hand, is built by intention, through clarity, strategic decisions, and consistent action. Most millionaires didn't inherit wealth; they created it step by step, proving that deliberate effort, not luck, produces lasting results.

My story, from immigrant beginnings to corporate professional to financial independence, is meant to show you what's possible. Retirement is about designing your own timeline, aligning your money with your values, and living purposefully in the years you are most capable of doing so.

Now it's your turn: start with one intentional choice and take the first step toward a life that is truly yours.

Wealth and Wisdom Declaration

These declarations anchor the truth that financial freedom is entering a life of vision, fulfillment, and purpose. Declaring them aloud as reminders that you are empowered to design your own timeline, rewrite your retirement story, and create a legacy that outlives you.

I boldly declare:

This is my era of divine design and disciplined destiny.

I rise as a visionary builder, crafting my financial freedom with divine wisdom, kingdom courage, and relentless faith.

I am designing my freedom now; with vision, discipline, and courage to start.

I am not enslaved by the world's system, but I function by heaven's economy.

My work is not my worth; my identity is anchored in God.

My profession is a platform, not a prison. Through it, I release impact, multiply value, and expand kingdom influence.

I reject the limitation of man-made timelines.

I will not wait for retirement to live.

I live fully now, led by divine purpose and sustained by divine provision.

I am empowered to create multiple streams of income that fund freedom, purpose, and legacy.

I operate in supernatural intelligence, divine innovation, and wealth strategies that defy logic.

I steward my finances with excellence, integrity, and insight.

My hands are blessed, my mind is sharp, my steps are ordered.

The wealth I manage today will outlive me tomorrow.

Early retirement is not my escape, it is my elevation.

It is the platform for purpose, peace, and prophetic productivity.

I am disciplined, intentional, and creative.

I use my gifts to generate wealth and to advance God's Kingdom on earth.

Every seed I sow multiplies in wisdom, influence, and impact.

I refuse scarcity thinking. I break covenant with lack.

I align my economy with heaven's overflow.

I attract divine opportunities and steward them faithfully.

I choose to live abundantly today, not someday.

I live with joy, not pressure; I build with grace, not grind.

Every financial step I take is aligned with divine timing and purpose.

My financial independence is not self-made—it is Spirit-led.

Through me, nations will learn financial wisdom, families will prosper, and generations will remember the faithfulness of God.

I am a prophetic picture of what divine design can do through human diligence.

I am FIRE'D UP!

I am designing the life I deserve, funded by the wealth I create. Amen

Chapter

Two

OVERCOMING
SCARCITY MINDSET

Y ou have just seen how a single decision, backed by discipline, multiple income streams, and a vision anchored in faith, can rewrite a life. Chapter 1 closed with a truth most of us never hear at work: your retirement timeline is yours to design. But design begins in the mind. Before the numbers shift, the narrative must. This chapter marks the beginning of a new narrative.

"Wealth begins in the mind. Until you shift your beliefs, no amount of money will ever feel like enough."

— Omolola Oyewumi.

Mindset: The Inner Revolution

The journey to financial independence begins long before the money arrives. It starts in the quiet shift of how you think, how you see possibilities, how you make choices, and how you commit to a different future. Wealth creation is first an internal revolution, a shift in mindset before it manifests externally. Yet, for many of us, particularly individuals from modest backgrounds, this internal journey involves overcoming deeply ingrained beliefs about scarcity.

You can earn six or seven figures a year and still live in fear, chasing "more" but never truly feeling secure. I've seen doctors, engineers, and tech professionals who look successful on paper, yet quietly drown in financial anxiety. Why? Because the scarcity mindset silently dictates their decisions.

These beliefs whisper quietly yet persistently:

● *"There's never enough."*

● *"Wealth is not for people like us."*

● *"Money is hard to earn."*

● *Etc.*

Such mindset barriers significantly impede wealth-building efforts, limiting not only financial success but also the quality of our lives. Your life is as good as your mindset. Recognizing and overcoming these barriers is vital for sustainable growth. As renowned author Stephen Covey once stated:

"Most people are deeply scripted in what I call the scarcity mentality. They see life as having only so much, as though there were only one pie out there."

A scarcity mindset is that inner voice telling you to cling tightly to money, fear change, hoard resources, or stay stuck in a job you dislike simply because it "pays well." It prevents you from investing, starting businesses, or building multiple income streams. It keeps you in survival mode, even when you already have enough to thrive.

Here's the truth: you cannot achieve financial independence if you remain trapped in scarcity.

Early retirement and true financial freedom demand boldness. It requires vision. It requires the courage to say, "I will create a life of freedom; not just for me, but for the generations after me." That courage begins with transforming your mindset and overcoming scarcity.

Understanding the Scarcity Mindset

The scarcity mindset is a mental programming rooted in fear, limitation, and a sense of lack. It is the belief that resources, money, opportunities, and time are never enough, forcing us to make choices from a place of constraint.

Psychologists Mullainathan and Shafir, in their book

Scarcity: Why Having Too Little Means So Much, explain that scarcity literally taxes the brain. When you believe resources are limited, your cognitive bandwidth narrows. You make shortsighted decisions, cling to "safe" routines, and sabotage your long-term goals, all while convincing yourself you're just being prudent.

Here are signs you may be operating with a scarcity mindset:

• You constantly fear running out, even with savings in the bank.

• You stay in unfulfilling jobs because you believe a steady paycheck is safer than taking a leap.

• You delay investing or wealth-building out of fear of loss.

• You underprice your skills or hesitate to ask for more, because you are scared people will say no.

• You feel guilt for desiring financial abundance, as if wanting more is wrong.

Sound familiar? For many of us, these patterns trace back to cultural scripts. While growing up, I constantly heard: "Cut your coat according to your size." "Don't reach for what is above you." "Money doesn't grow on trees." These sayings taught us to shrink dreams rather than stretch our imagination. Even when I earned well in the U.S., those childhood voices echoed sometimes: "Be careful. Don't lose it. Don't aim too high."

But here is the truth: those scripts are not universal laws. They are simply borrowed beliefs, and like any belief, they can be rewritten. The consequences of not rewriting them are costly. According to research published in the Harvard Business Review, people operating with financial scarcity are more likely to take on predatory loans, avoid long-term investing, and remain trapped in paycheck-to-paycheck cycles.

Scarcity is not "safe." It is expensive. It robs you of confidence, keeps you playing small, and delays your independence. And perhaps the most significant cost is that it makes financial freedom feel impossible. You could be earning enough to thrive yet still believe you can only survive. You could be on the edge of opportunity yet retreat into comfort because fear screams louder than vision. But abundance whispers louder if you let it.

The consequences of scarcity thinking

Most people are unaware of this, but scarcity is far more expensive than it appears. Not just in dollars, but in opportunities, in relationships, in health, and the very quality of life you could be enjoying. It silently erodes potential long before it touches your bank account.

Research proves it. A Harvard Business Review study reveals that individuals operating under financial scarcity tend to make poorer long-term decisions, such as taking high-interest loans, cashing out retirement accounts prematurely, and avoiding investment altogether. Why?

Because their mental bandwidth is consumed by the need for survival. Scarcity doesn't just drain your wallet; it hijacks your brain. It narrows your focus, making it nearly impossible to think beyond the immediate, even when long-term prosperity is within reach.

When you live under the weight of scarcity, confidence begins to slip almost imperceptibly. You hesitate to raise your hand for opportunities, fearing failure or rejection. You avoid negotiating for higher pay because asking feels too risky. Ideas that could blossom into thriving businesses or new streams of income are silenced by the quiet voice of fear, convincing you that playing small is safer.

Scarcity has a way of quietly shrinking your world. Instead of daring to expand your paycheck to align with your dreams, you trim your dreams to fit the paycheck you already have. The ambitions that once energized you begin to feel unattainable, so you settle for less. Your vision narrows, your choices contract, and the life you could have imagined starts to feel out of reach.

It pushes you into cycles of overwork and under-earning. You convince yourself that the only way forward is to grind harder, pouring in longer hours that never quite translate into the income or freedom you imagined.

And then there's the quiet delay. "I'll start tomorrow" becomes a mantra that silently adds years to your FIRE timeline. The dream of financial independence continues to recede further.

Scarcity is a thief masquerading as caution. It steals your future while tricking you into believing you're being cautious. It whispers, "Don't invest, it's too risky." Yet by not investing, you lose decades of compound growth. It says, "Stay in this job, it's secure." Yet by staying, you miss opportunities to build wealth aligned with your purpose. Scarcity convinces you that clinging to the familiar is safe when in reality, it is the riskiest choice of all.

I've seen this over and over: professionals earning multiple six figures who still live paycheck to paycheck. They don't lack income; they lack belief. They haven't shifted from scarcity to abundance. They don't believe they can have wealth and joy, impact, and freedom. They think they must choose between hustle and happiness, when abundance allows them to design both. Scarcity is not just a mindset; it is a slow, costly tax on your life. It steals time, energy, and hope, convincing you that survival is all you can hope for when abundance could have been yours all along.

Here is the hard truth: if you don't confront scarcity head-on, you will keep running on the treadmill of "enough someday." You tell yourself that once you earn a little more, save a little more, or invest a little more, then freedom will arrive. But "someday" is a mirage; it keeps moving further away the more you chase it without addressing the mindset that holds you back.

While you are waiting for "enough," life continues. Time with your family slips by. Experiences pass unclaimed.

Opportunities to grow, invest, or create additional income are missed. The energy and creativity you could pour into building wealth are siphoned off by worry and doubt.

Scarcity delays your freedom and denies it. The longer you let it dictate your choices, the more you convince yourself that true financial independence is a luxury meant for others, not for you.

The FIRE Lens: Why Mindset Is Everything

The first step to breaking free from scarcity is realizing that abundance is not a number; abundance is a mindset. Many believe they will feel abundant once they have saved or earned enough, but the truth is the opposite: you must think abundantly long before the evidence shows up. That shift changes everything.

Scarcity Thinking	Abundance Thinking
"I need to work until 65"	*"I can retire as soon as I become financially free."*
"I can only earn from my job" *passions, and investments."*	*"I can earn from my skills,*
"I can't afford that." *and sustainably?"*	*"How can I afford that, wisely*
"What if I lose everything?" *and impact?"*	*"What if I gain time, freedom,*

The FIRE Lens requires four mindset shifts that changed my life and can transform yours.

1. Believe that Money Is Unlimited

Scarcity teaches that money is a fixed pie, that there is only so much to go around, and if someone else takes a slice, your share gets smaller. It convinces you that wealth is limited, that opportunities are rare, and that financial security comes from guarding what you already have rather than creating more.

Abundance, on the other hand, operates on a completely different principle. Abundance knows money is created through value, not rationed by need. It knows that money is not a zero-sum game; it is created through value, effort, and contribution, and not rationed by need. Every day, wealth circulates through salaries, investments, and opportunities, flowing to those who produce, serve, and innovate. Your wealth does not take from anyone else; it expands when you create and contribute.

Jim Rohn captured this perfectly: *"The universe doesn't reward need. It rewards value."* Internalize that, and everything changes. Fear no longer drives your decisions. Instead of hoarding or hesitating, you start to see possibilities. You recognize that offering your skills, your knowledge, and your creativity is the pathway to financial growth.

When you embrace abundance, you realize that financial

growth is not about luck or inheritance; it's about consistently producing value and allowing that value to multiply in the world. Your mindset shifts from protection to creation, from worry to opportunity, and from scarcity to a confidence that your efforts can expand not just your wealth, but your influence, freedom, and impact.

2. Embrace the power of delayed gratification

Scarcity craves instant comfort. Abundance plays the long game. Delayed gratification is your secret financial weapon. It is the discipline to say a smaller "no" today to say a far greater "yes" tomorrow.

In my journey, this meant skipping vacations to build assets, investing in financial literacy while others bought luxuries, and choosing growth over comfort. Every sacrifice became a deposit into my future freedom.

The science is clear: the famous Stanford Marshmallow Experiment demonstrated that children who resisted an immediate reward in exchange for a larger one later exhibited stronger self-control, higher achievement, and better financial habits. Decades later, researchers confirmed it: Adults who consistently practice delayed gratification accumulate nearly double the wealth of those who do not (Journal of Economic Psychology, 2018).

The truth is that delayed gratification is not deprivation but a strategy. It requires discipline, but it rewards you with exponential returns in freedom, wealth, and fulfillment.

"Abundance trusts tomorrow enough to discipline today."
– Omolola Oyewumi

3. Expand your Vision

You cannot move toward what you cannot see. Abundance demands that you picture yourself already free from financial stress. To live free from financial stress, you must first imagine it as real. Picture your mornings unhurried, waking without dread or obligation, filled with time for reflection, family, and the work that energizes you. See your relationships strengthened, not strained by money worries. Visualize your work as a source of purpose, not pressure, where opportunities align with your skills, passions, and values, rather than forcing you into a state of survival mode. These images prime your mind to create what it repeatedly sees. Daily affirmations act as anchors for this vision, keeping it alive and tangible even when scarcity tries to creep in.

4. Master your financial habits

A mindset without habits will not foster independence. Thinking abundantly is not enough on its own; it must be paired with intentional, consistent action. Abundance shows up in practice. It is evident in the small but disciplined choices you make every day that compound over time into financial freedom.

Forecasting, not fearful budgeting. Forecasting rather than fearful budgeting is one of the first habits to develop. Instead of anxiously tracking every dollar to avoid loss, you anticipate expenses, plan for opportunities, and make money work for you. You see where it's going, how it can grow, and how it can serve your long-term vision.

Saving to invest, not to hoard. Saving to invest, rather than hoarding, is another critical practice. Money kept idle may feel safe, but it does not multiply. By purposefully directing funds into investments, assets, and ventures, you create opportunities for wealth to grow exponentially. You are no longer a passive recipient of income; you become a steward, a creator, and a driver of your financial future.

Paying yourself first before spending elsewhere. Paying yourself first, setting aside a portion of income before expenses, is a mindset shift. It signals that your future, your freedom, and your goals take priority. This simple act compounds over time, ensuring that wealth builds steadily instead of being consumed by urgent but less important needs.

Building multiple income streams so no single source defines your future.

Building multiple income streams transforms risk into resilience. Relying on a single paycheck leaves you vulnerable to layoffs, reorganizations, or market shifts. Creating multiple avenues for earning, whether through investments, consulting, real estate, or side ventures, provides both security and flexibility. Each stream reinforces the others, creating a safety net that allows you to take bold steps toward your vision without fear.

These habits, repeated consistently, form the foundation of lasting freedom. They turn abstract intentions into concrete results. The difference between dreaming about financial independence and achieving it lies entirely in this bridge between mindset and action.

Rewiring for abundance is not a one-time event; it is a daily choice. To see possibilities instead of limitations. To prioritize the future over fleeting comfort. To imagine boldly and act consistently. When you live from this place, opportunities flow, often faster than you ever believed possible.

"Abundance is not about what you have, it is about how you think, how you choose, and how you act. When your mindset aligns with abundance, money becomes a servant to your vision, not a master of your fear."

– Omolola Oyewumi

From Fear to Freedom: Choosing Abundance

When my company announced a reorganization, I was presented with the "safe" choice: interview for another role, keep the paycheck, maintain the benefits. On paper, it made perfect sense. But I knew something deeper—

choosing comfort would come at the cost of my freedom.

Fear tried to claim the moment, whispering its familiar doubts:

• *"What if you never make enough again?"*

• *"What if your business fails?"*

• *"You're a mom with kids, what will happen without a steady paycheck?"*

In fact, the hardest whisper of all: "Are you being reckless?"

Fear had a strong case. Yet I had done the work. Years of building multiple income streams, real estate, writing, coaching, insurance, and financial planning, had prepared me for this exact season. I had learned, tested, and saved deliberately, and I am still saving. Walking away from Microsoft was not an easy decision. The silence after leaving felt deafening: no paycheck, no emails, no manager telling me what to do. But that silence created space. Space to hear God's direction.

Space to build solutions. Space to design a life aligned with my values. For four months, I was on sabbatical, pouring only into my children, which was very fulfilling.

And I discovered this truth: freedom is not the absence of work, but the presence of purpose.

My story is not unique. The same shift has fueled the lives of people we all admire:

• Oprah Winfrey grew up in poverty so deep she wore dresses made from potato sacks. Scarcity surrounded her, but she refused to let it define her. Through education and affirmations, she rewrote her internal script. Today, with a net worth of over $2 billion, she reminds us: "Be thankful for what you have; you will end up having more. If you concentrate on what you do not have, you will never, ever have enough."

• Tony Robbins faced eviction notices and hunger as a child. His early beliefs echoed scarcity: "We do not have enough. Wealth is unattainable." Instead of surrendering, he immersed himself in mentors and learning, reprogramming his focus. His mantra: "Where focus goes, energy flows. Focus on abundance, and abundance will follow."

• Warren Buffett grew up modestly but chose his environment carefully. He surrounded himself with abundance-minded thinkers, insisting, "You will move in the direction of the people you associate with. Choose carefully." That intentional choice became part of the foundation for one of the greatest fortunes in history.

The thread is clear: abundance begins within but grows through practice. For me, it meant walking away from a paycheck to walk into purpose. For Oprah, Robbins, and Buffett, it meant rewriting their beliefs, reprogramming their focus, and curating environments that enabled them to thrive. For you, it may mean choosing courage over comfort and possibility over fear.

Abundance is a decision; the moment you choose it, everything begins to shift. Scarcity will always whisper, but abundance has the final word, if you are willing to listen.

Action Steps

Rewiring for Abundance

Scarcity begins in the mind, and abundance begins with practice. Here are your first steps to rewire your mindset and start living from a place of possibility:

- Identify scarcity scripts. Write down the top three money beliefs you inherited.

- Reframe them. Replace each script with an abundance belief ("Money flows to me through service and value", "I can build wealth with purpose", etc.).

- Practice delayed gratification. Choose one expense this week to postpone and redirect that money into savings or investments. Prove to yourself that waiting creates freedom.

- Affirm abundance daily. Repeat affirmations morning and night: "Abundance is my birthright. Money is a tool. I retire on my own terms."

- Visualize your abundant life. Spend five minutes daily picturing your life without scarcity. What does your morning look like? Who are you with? What are you doing?

- Take one bold step. Whether it is opening an

investment account, starting a side gig, or raising your rates, act from abundance, not fear.

Chapter Summary

Scarcity is both a financial condition and a mental prison. It whispers that safety is found in clinging tightly, but it steals confidence, shrinks dreams, and delays financial independence. Scarcity convinces us to stay small when, in truth, it robs us of the future we could create.

Abundance begins before the money arrives. It is first a mindset, then a balance sheet. It is the belief that tomorrow can be bigger than today, that money is created, not rationed, and that delayed gratification is not deprivation but a pathway to freedom. Abundance expands your vision, fuels your faith, and grounds your financial habits in purpose.

My decision to leave corporate at 40 was about breaking free from fear and choosing alignment with faith, legacy, vision, and possibility. That same choice is available to you. Scarcity may shout, but abundance whispers louder if you are willing to listen.

Wealth and Wisdom Declaration

Scarcity is silenced by faith and abundance is activated by choice. Speak these declarations daily to renew your mind, strengthen your courage, and position yourself to experience true financial freedom and fulfillment.

I boldly decree:

I awaken to the abundance that is already mine.

My mind is renewed, my vision enlarged, and my spirit aligned with divine prosperity.

I decree that abundant thoughts shape my reality, and I expect abundant outcomes in every area of my life.

Scarcity no longer has power over me.

Every limiting belief, fear, and lie of insufficiency is uprooted from my consciousness.

I release lack from my spirit and welcome overflow into my atmosphere.

I choose abundance over anxiety.

I see money as a tool for impact, not an idol of identity.

I believe that tomorrow holds greater possibility than today because I walk with the God of increase.

I affirm that my vision is not small.

I expand it daily because I serve an unlimited God.

I dream without fear, plan with wisdom, and execute with excellence.

I confess that I embrace divine discipline and delayed gratification.

I do not despise process, for I know that patience perfects promise.

Every delay is divine development, preparing me for durable success.

I affirm that I can have both wealth and joy, prosperity and peace, financial freedom, and fulfillment; all together.

I decree that I reject the false dichotomy between hustle and happiness.

I walk in the divine rhythm where purpose births profit and peace guards' progress.

I declare that I am a creator, an answer to my generation.

Solutions flow from me with divine intelligence.

Wealth flows to me as I serve with value, purpose, and vision.

I am a vessel of wisdom, a carrier of creativity, and a magnet for divine opportunities.

I affirm that I am bold, courageous, and unafraid to take risks aligned with wisdom and guided by purpose.

I do not shrink back in fear; I rise in faith.

My steps are ordered, my mind is sound, and my results are supernatural.

I decree that abundance is my covenant birthright.

I live in overflow, not overwhelm.

I retire on my terms; with joy, with peace, and with purpose fulfilled.

From this day forward, my life reflects heaven's economy.

My mindset is multiplied, my resources are replenished, and my future overflows with possibility.

I am FIRE'D Up for abundance.

I am anchored in wisdom.

I am advancing with grace.

I live in divine sufficiency, where nothing is missing, nothing is lacking, and nothing is broken. Amen.

Chapter
Three

FULFILLMENT BEYOND THE PAYCHECK

You have already seen that your FIRE timeline is yours to design, and that true wealth begins in the mind. Once you understand that freedom isn't tied to a particular age, and you let go of the scarcity beliefs that keep many people trapped, a deeper question emerges: What are you building this life for?

Because without that answer, even financial freedom can start to feel aimless. You can optimize every account, hit every milestone, and still find yourself pouring energy into goals that do not move you forward. The work never really stops; it just changes form. You are still striving, still busy, but now without a clear target. It becomes another version of working in vain, more spreadsheets, more hustle, yet no deeper satisfaction because the effort is not anchored to meaning.

Financial independence without fulfillment is like tending a garden with no seeds. You can till the soil, water it faithfully, and bask in the sun every day, but if you never plant meaning, nothing lasting will grow. Have seen too many high-achieving professionals reach their financial goals only to realize they never sowed peace, joy, or legacy. They worked tirelessly to achieve financial freedom, but never paused to define what joy, rest, or fulfillment would look like once they arrived. Without that clarity, their success yielded abundance but no sense of satisfaction or fulfillment.

Those who plant with intention, whether through family, finances, faith, creativity, or contribution, see their efforts blossom in ways that feel deeply satisfying. Their resources begin to work toward clearly defined goals, not vague notions of success. In the real sense, wealth is simply the soil, the water, and the light necessary for planting, not harvesting. The real fruit meant to be yielded is fulfillment. The goal was never just to make more money, but to harness resources that empower us to create, give, and live a life full of impact.

True joy is found in what wealth makes possible. Wealth is meant to empower you to create, to give, and to live with intention. When resources are aligned with purpose, they multiply their impact. They become the foundation for ideas that uplift others and for generosity that outlives us, empowering the next generation.

For those seeking FIRE, defining fulfillment absolutely matters. Clarity about what fulfillment means to you is as critical as learning the financial principles that secure independence. Just as compound interest multiplies your money over time, a clear vision multiplies the impact of every decision you make. Without it, financial freedom can become another version of busyness, a restless pursuit of "more" with no true north.

Some reach their "number," step away from work, and within months find themselves anxious, uninspired, or drifting back to what they once escaped, not necessarily for money, but because they crave purpose. FIRE without a vision can be as dangerous as living paycheck to paycheck. One may have money in the bank, but both share the same root problem: a lack of direction. Without a clear sense of purpose, early retirement can become another form of striving.

Some who raced towards FIRE reached their number and still found themselves unfulfilled. They mastered the mechanics of wealth but never defined what that wealth was supposed to serve. So, they returned to work, not out of necessity, but to reclaim the meaning that drifted away in the pursuit of the goal itself.

Others, however, aligned their lives with their values long before financial independence. These groups defined fulfillment early and built toward it intentionally. Their work stopped being a cage and became an expression of their calling and purpose. They were not simply leaving their jobs to escape; they were moving toward a life that energized and empowered them.

As Franklin D. Roosevelt said,

"Happiness is not in the mere possession of money; it lies in the joy of achievement, in the thrill of creative effort."

Wealth, then, is the resource that allows us to do meaningful work, create, give, and live fully in purpose, and then we get the reward. So, before we talk about how to earn, save, or invest better, let's pause and reflect:

What lights you up? What gives your days a sense of meaning? If money were no longer a factor, what would you keep showing up for simply because it brings you joy and purpose?

By the end of this chapter, you will not only define fulfillment for yourself but also see how to align your financial strategy with it, so your wealth does not just afford you financial freedom but also funds a life of joy, purpose, and lasting impact.

Defining and Discovering Your Fulfillment

Fulfillment is deeply personal. No two people will define it the same way. For one person, it may be mentoring the next generation. For another, fulfillment may be having the liberty to write a novel in a cabin by a quiet lake, uninterrupted. For someone else, traveling the world and learning new languages is what produces a deep sense of satisfaction.

There is no universal formula because fulfillment grows from the values that shape who you are. Fulfillment is not limited to a job title or a number in your account, though those things can certainly be part of it. The danger comes when fulfillment is only attached to them; when a promotion, a paycheck, or recognition at work becomes the sole measure of meaning.

Many people spend years building careers that look successful on paper, only to realize later that the sense of purpose they were chasing can't be found in a title. While work and financial stability are important, fulfillment often grows out of something deeper: the alignment between your values, your time, and your everyday rhythm. It's found in how you live, not just in what you do or the titles you have.

For me, the FIRE'D UP Queen, fulfillment means helping people, professionals, and individuals in their careers, step into a life where money is no longer a source of stress but a tool for freedom. It is seeing professionals build wealth for themselves and their families, not just to survive, but to thrive. It is seeing missionary kids get a good education so their parents can continue serving God and proclaiming the Gospel.

Being the FIRE'D UP Queen goes beyond simply holding a title. Fulfillment is in what it represents: empowering others to step into confidence, purpose, and freedom. Stepping away from corporate life opened the door to the work I felt truly called to. My joy comes from seeing others rise, rewrite their financial stories, and walk in alignment with what God has called them to do. This is my version of fulfillment. Yours will take a different shape, and that is the beauty of it.

Fulfillment in Action

Fulfillment looks different for everyone, but when it's lived out with purpose, it's unmistakable. You can see it in the way people work, create, and give. Consider these two powerful examples of what fulfillment looks like in practice:

Richard Branson's Adventure Spirit

For Richard, wealth has never been about quiet luxury or status. From Virgin Records to Virgin Galactic, he has used his business and success as an opportunity for greater creativity and curiosity. Each new venture reflects his desire to push boundaries and to profit from them. From crossing oceans and circling the globe in balloons to reaching for space, Branson treats wealth as permission to keep exploring. His story teaches us that when wealth supports passion, it becomes a launchpad for adventure, innovation, and joy.

Hamdi Ulukaya's Purpose-Driven Success

When Turkish immigrant Hamdi Ulukaya founded

Chobani, he was not just starting a yogurt company; he was building something designed to create lasting impact. He turned his business into a platform for social good by sharing profits with employees, offering paid parental leave, and intentionally hiring refugees to help rebuild their lives. His vision was simple but transformative: to prove that business could serve people, not just shareholders, and that success has greater meaning when it improves others' lives.

For Ulukaya, wealth is opportunity and dignity. His journey shows us that fulfillment is found when success opens doors for others. This is a reminder that true prosperity multiplies beyond income, but also in impact.

Both stories point to a larger truth: fulfillment is never one-size-fits-all, but it often grows from the same foundations: Purpose, Growth, Contribution, and Connection. Whether you are going after adventure like Branson, creating opportunities like Ulukaya, or defining fulfillment in your own unique way, these four dimensions sustain every version of a fulfilled life.

The Four Dimensions of Fulfillment

Though fulfillment takes on many forms, the foundation remains remarkably consistent. Across careers, cultures, and seasons, the lives that feel most rewarding are built on four enduring dimensions: Purpose, Growth, Contribution, and Connection. These are the same pillars that guide each of us toward meaning and balance.

Think of these four dimensions as the coordinates that keep your life balanced. They give direction when you are unsure of what comes next and offer perspective when the world tells you that success is only about gaining more or reaching the perfect "number". Ignore one, and you may find yourself moving fast but drifting off course. But when they work together, your wealth, time, and energy start to point toward a life that feels aligned, purposeful, and whole.

1. *Purpose: The "Why" Behind What You Do*

Purpose is the fuel that keeps you moving when challenges in life arise. It's the reason you get out of bed each morning and the thing that keeps you anchored when things feel uncertain. Without purpose, even financial independence can start to feel like an endless weekend, lacking real direction or meaning.

When purpose isn't guiding your choices, it's easy to lose momentum and desire to continue pursuing your goals. The days begin to blur together, and even the freedom you once longed for can leave you feeling empty. Purpose is essentially the why behind the decisions you make every day; the driving force that shapes how you spend your time, use your money, and direct your energy. When you find your "why", even ordinary choices begin to feel more meaningful.

I'll never forget one client I mentored. She was a mid-career professional from Nigeria who reached her financial independence goal and decided that financial freedom was not an ending, but the beginning of a journey into purposeful living. She did not simply walk away from work; she poured her time and resources into starting a STEM mentorship program for young African girls.

Her story stayed with me because it was an example of what happens when purpose and financial freedom finally meet. The joy she found was not just in starting a program and watching it grow, but in realizing that her financial independence had given her the freedom to direct her resources towards a legacy that would outlive her. Watching the girls discover new confidence and possibilities through her STEM program brought her a level of fulfillment that far outweighed the thrill of hitting her financial milestone.

I want to reiterate that this kind of alignment does not happen by chance. It takes time, honesty, and a willingness to pause long enough to ask what truly matters. Most people move so fast, chasing the next goal, that they never stop to think where it is all leading to. Throughout my career, I have seen again and again that the most powerful transformations happen when resources begin to flow toward purpose.

That's often the moment fulfillment finally becomes a reality. It allows you to build with intention and opens doors to possibilities you may never have imagined before. When you have defined your "why," money becomes the resource that makes it possible; it allows you to step into meaningful work, creative ventures, or missions that light you up, without the constant weight of financial pressure.

2. *Growth: Opportunities to Learn, Improve, and Expand*

Humans are designed to grow. We come alive when we stretch beyond our comfort zones and what's familiar, which might be learning a new skill, embracing a creative challenge, or exploring new territory in your career or passions.

Without growth, even the best-planned life can start to feel repetitive. I have seen it happen, and at times, I have felt it too, when the same routines that once brought comfort begin to dull your curiosity. The habits that built your security can slowly turn into limitations if you are not intentional about continuing to grow. Real growth often begins in those uneasy moments when you sense that what once served you cannot take you where you are meant to go next.

I once worked with a client who retired at forty-five after reaching her financial independence goal. She began exploring photography, not as a new career, but simply to keep learning and creating. What started as a simple hobby evolved into a thriving travel photography business. It is important to know that growth is not restricted to just professional development; it can find expression in areas of life we rarely think about, in curiosity, in small creative pursuits, or in the effort to see familiar things differently.

That is what growth does; it keeps life vibrant long after the structure of the corporate life fades. It gives shape to your days and keeps you curious about what is still possible. And yes, growth also requires intention and investment, financial in time, and in commitment. Sometimes it looks like taking time off to learn a new language, traveling to see the world differently, pursuing a long-delayed certification, or finally making space for something you've always wanted to do. Each step toward growth is an opportunity to expand your worldview and enrich your independence.

3. *Contribution: Giving and Leaving a Legacy*

Contribution is what gives success meaning. It is the moment your resources, your time, your money, your experience, start to move beyond you and make a difference in someone else's life. Sometimes that looks like funding a scholarship, mentoring a young professional, or even helping a family member take the next step forward.

Earlier, I shared the story of Hamdi Ulukaya, the founder of Chobani. His approach to business still stands out to me because it captures the heart of contribution. He didn't wait until he succeeded to start giving. He built generosity into the foundation of his work. That kind of mindset changes how we think about wealth. It shows that contribution isn't something we add on once we've "made it"; it can be woven into the way we live, lead, and build from the start.

What makes contribution so powerful is the ripple effect it creates, often in ways we never see.

One act of generosity can spark something in someone else, a decision to give, to volunteer, or to pay it forward in their own way. I have watched people underestimate how far their impact travels simply because they couldn't measure it outright. But the truth is, generosity rarely ends where it starts. A scholarship inspires another to mentor. A donation fuels a cause that touches hundreds. Even a small gesture of support can shift the direction of someone's story. That's the subtle strength of giving: it multiplies beyond our reach. We may never know the full extent of it, but that's part of what makes it so powerful.

I have seen that same principle reflected in the lives of many professionals I have worked with. Some have funded scholarships for first-generation students, launched women's entrepreneurship funds, and sponsored clean water projects abroad. The common thread is that their giving reflects what they value most.

When generosity flows from a place of alignment, instead of feeling like a loss, it feels natural. You stop giving out of duty and start giving out of gratitude, and success becomes a tool for empowering those around you. Contribution is where legacy begins. It is found in the people who are impacted by your generosity and in the difference that continues long after you have given.

4. *Connection: Relationships That Nourish Your Soul*

At the end of life, most people do not wish they had spent more time in the office. What they often long for is more time with the people they love. Connection is about nurturing the relationships that matter most to us: family, friends, community, and those who truly see and support you.

Money can open doors, but it cannot replace the warmth of being known and loved. The laughter around the dinner table, the long talk after a busy day, the feeling of being fully present with people who matter, those are the things that outlast many professional milestones and become a lasting source of joy.

There was a time in my life when I struggled with this balance. I was working hard, providing for my family, and reaching every goal I had set, but I noticed the growing distance between me and my children. Long days and constant deadlines left little room for the moments that truly mattered. Financial freedom, for me, was not just about stepping away from that pace; it was about reclaiming time to show up, to listen, and to be fully present with my children.

Now, the memories I treasure most come from everyday moments of cooking together, baking, laughing at inside jokes, or simply being there when it counts. That's what fulfillment looks like in practice: using the time and resources you've worked hard for to nurture the relationships that give life its meaning.

FIRE gives back your most precious resource: time. Time to be present, to slow down, and to truly connect with the people you love. When used with intention, that time allows you to strengthen bonds, create memories, and build the support systems that make life richer than any paycheck. For me, it meant being present again for my children in ways I couldn't when work consumed my attention, but it can also look like taking parents on the trip they've always dreamed of, hosting friends and family, surprising a spouse with a getaway, or simply being more present at home.

Money That Works for You

Every financial plan should tell a story that reaches beyond numbers. Behind every goal should be a vision for the kind of life those numbers make possible, one filled with peace, purpose, and lasting impact. Money, on its own, is neutral. What gives it meaning is direction.

When your resources begin to move toward what matters most, they become tools for freedom. They create room for growth, generosity, and connection in ways possessions never can. Luxury fades; fulfillment doesn't. The excitement of new things wears off, but experiences continue to give back long after the moment has passed.

Experiences, however, return value again and again. They shape you, stay with you, and reveal how wealth finds its highest meaning in the memories and growth it makes possible.

The purpose of money is activation. It is meant to move, to flow toward the people and moments that give life depth. In the end, the real measure of wealth is how your resources have allowed you to live with joy, give with intention, and create meaningful connections, not what you own.

"The value of money is found in the life it enables."

— Omolola Oyewumi

Practical FIRE Application: Designing for Fulfillment

Your FIRE journey should fund more than your bills. It should help you build a life that feels whole and deeply aligned with what matters to you. That's why I encourage you to create what I call a Fulfillment Budget, money set aside intentionally to nurture the four dimensions that make life rich: Purpose, Growth, Contribution, and Connection.

Purpose

Direct a portion of your budget toward what fuels your calling. This could mean launching a mentorship program, developing a creative project, or bringing your business idea to life. Purpose spending allows your wealth to serve your deeper vision, turning financial independence into the freedom to create lasting impact.

Growth

Set aside funds for experiences that stretch you. Take a course, attend a retreat or conference, or explore a new place that challenges your perspective. Growth spending ensures that you continue to evolve, personally, creatively, and spiritually, long after the pursuit of financial freedom has been achieved.

Contribution

Dedicate part of your budget to giving in ways that reflect your values. That might mean supporting first-generation college students, funding a women's entrepreneurship initiative, or backing grassroots projects in your community. Contribution transforms financial capital into human capital, expanding the reach of your success far beyond yourself.

Connection

Reserve money for the relationships that give life meaning. This could be planning family trips, hosting gatherings, or simply making space in your calendar to be present with loved ones. Connection spending turns time and generosity into shared memories that outlast any purchase.

When your wealth flows intentionally through these four dimensions, it becomes movement, creating experiences, opportunities, and impact that extend well beyond numbers on a spreadsheet. Over time, your money begins to mirror your values. Professionals who have embraced this shift often say the same thing: when your giving and spending align with your deepest values, it doesn't feel like a cost. It feels like an investment in humanity, in legacy, and in a life well lived.

"Wealth is not to feed our egos, but to feed and clothe the hungry and to help people help themselves."

— Andrew Carnegie

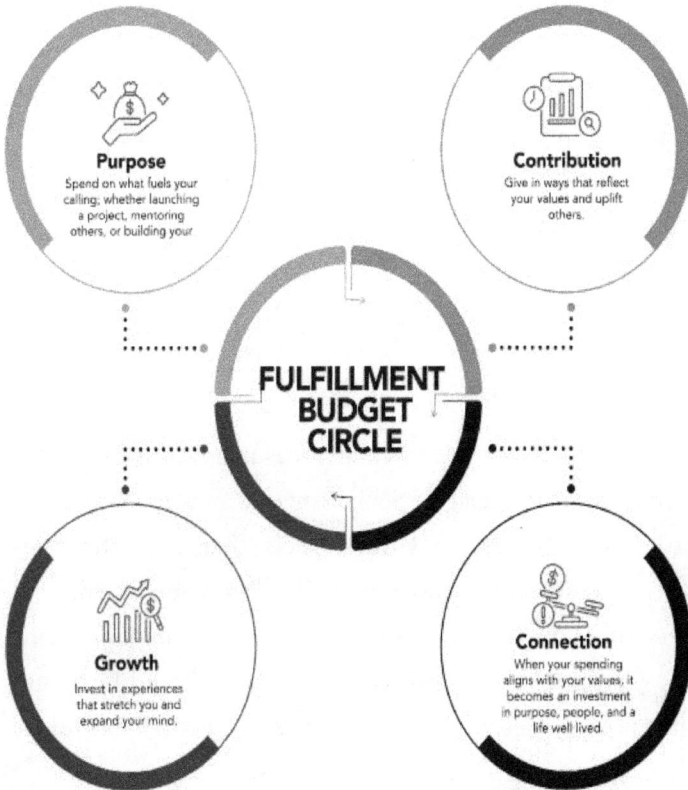

Purpose
Spend on what fuels your calling; whether launching a project, mentoring others, or building your

Contribution
Give in ways that reflect your values and uplift others.

FULFILLMENT BUDGET CIRCLE

Growth
Invest in experiences that stretch you and expand your mind.

Connection
When your spending aligns with your values, it becomes an investment in purpose, people, and a life well lived.

Common Fulfillment Pitfalls

Even with a clear vision, it's easy to drift off course. The path to financial independence is often full of distractions that can shift your focus away from what matters most. Keeping your goals front and center helps you recognize the difference between progress and distractions. Here are a few common traps that derail professionals on the FIRE path:

1. *The Shiny Object Syndrome*

New opportunities can feel exciting. Whether it's the latest investment trend, tech upgrade, or side hustle that promises quick results, not everything that glitters leads to growth. When you chase every new idea, you risk shifting your focus and losing sight of what truly matters. Fulfillment comes when your choices reflect your core values, not just passing excitement. If it does not serve your purpose or align with your values, it is clutter.

2. *The Comparison Trap*

Nothing steals joy faster than measuring your progress against someone else's. Social media makes this even harder, with endless highlight reels that blur the line between inspiration and insecurity. But your journey is yours alone. No two paths to financial independence will look the same, and that is exactly how it should be. True fulfillment comes when you measure success by your own values and not by someone else's milestones.

3. *Overwork Blindness*

Many people reach their Financial Independence (FI) number only to realize they have traded time, health, and relationships along the way. The danger is in thinking rest is something you earn later instead of something you practice now. It's essential to build in rest, play, and connection today; you don't have to delay living for a number. As Socrates once said, "Beware the barrenness of a busy life."

The truth is simple: money alone will never bring meaning. Numbers are meaningless unless you know what they are funding. When your wealth is directed with intention, it fuels purpose, growth, contribution, and connection. Without that clarity, it only amplifies emptiness.

Redefining Fulfillment: My Early Retirement Perspective

When people ask me what early retirement means, I tell them this: You can have millions in the bank, but if someone else's calendar still rules your days, you are not truly experiencing freedom.

For me, early retirement was never about never working again. I believe God designed us to create, to steward, and to add value. The real question is not whether we are to work or not work, but what kind of work are we choosing to do? No matter what industry we are in, our work is meant to align with our purpose, our faith, and our deepest values.

That is why I see retirement not as an escape, but as an expansion. Escape is about running from something: stress, burnout, or the feeling of being trapped in a cycle that no longer fulfills you. It can bring temporary relief, but it often leaves you searching for the next thing to fill the space.

Expansion, on the other hand, is about moving toward something greater. It is widening of life itself, more space to live with intention, more energy to invest in what truly matters, and the freedom to live the kind of life God always intended. But I didn't always know this.

By every external measure, I had "made it." I had a respected corporate role at Microsoft. An advanced degree. A six-figure salary and benefits. If you saw my resume, it looked like the definition of success. But while what I had built looked like success, it surprisingly did not feel the way I thought it would. Somewhere between the deadlines and the meetings, I lost the part of myself that used to dream.

Most days, I went through the motions, producing results that mattered to the company but left me feeling detached from my own sense of purpose. There was an aching I felt inside that I couldn't explain. My schedule was full, yet I couldn't shake the feeling that I was missing something essential. I had money, security, and status, but very little joy or fulfillment.

One evening, I finally decided to face the truth. I realized I had built a life that looked great on paper but didn't fulfill me. I was not unhappy, but I wasn't whole either. I had financial security in my own definition, but I was starved of meaning and purpose. That night, I gave myself permission to stop striving and to redefine what fulfillment meant to me. I began writing my non-negotiables, the things I wanted to build my life around and the parts of myself I refused to keep sacrificing for work:

• My work must create impact, especially for professionals navigating financial freedom.

• My family must be at the center of God's purpose and my life, not squeezed into the margins.

• I must have space to mentor, write, speak, and inspire others through my story.

• I will travel and experience the world because life is meant to be lived in full color.

That list became my compass. Money gave me options, but clarity gave me direction. Along the way, I realized something deeper: Wealthness, the union of wellness and wealth, is my mantra. True prosperity means honoring your health, your faith, and your purpose with the same intentionality you give your finances. There is little value in overworking to build wealth if your health breaks down or if you are too exhausted to enjoy what you have built. When that happens, your resources often end up paying for the rest you denied yourself earlier.

Wealthness is about integration. When wellness and wealth

move in the same direction, money becomes a support system for the life God intended, not a replacement for it.

For me, early retirement is about stepping into something larger. A life designed with purpose, growth, contribution, and connection at its core. That was the day I redefined fulfillment, and that is the gift I now help others claim: the freedom to design fulfillment not someday, but now.

Action Steps

Designing Your Fulfillment Beyond the Paycheck

Knowledge is powerful, but real transformation happens through action. Understanding these principles is the first step; living them out is what brings change. The steps below are meant to help you take what you have learned and start applying it in a way that feels real and personal. My hope is that as you work through them, you begin to see fulfillment not as a distant goal, but as something you can build right where you are.

List Your Joy Triggers

Write down the top three activities that make you feel most alive.

Think about the moments when time seems to disappear, and you end the day feeling energized and at peace. These are your north stars for how you should spend your money and your time. They point you back to what matters most when life gets busy or goals start to blur.

Identify Your Fulfillment Dimensions

Choose the two or three dimensions that matter most right now: Purpose, Growth, Contribution, or Connection.

Write one sentence for each about why it matters to you and how you want to live it out. This helps clarify where to focus your energy and resources in this season of your life.

Design Your Freedom Day

Imagine waking up tomorrow completely financially independent. No paycheck and no obligations. What would your perfect day look like from morning to night? Write it down in detail. That vision is what your FIRE plan should support and make possible.

Create a Fulfillment Fund

Open a separate account or set aside a portion of your savings for experiences, giving opportunities, and personal growth opportunities that bring you joy. Start small, even if it's just $50 a month. The amount matters less than the intention behind it.

Audit Your Calendar

Look at your week ahead and notice one thing that drains you. Replace it with something that aligns with your joy triggers or fulfillment dimensions. Often, we move from task to task without realizing how certain habits or commitments drain our energy. Taking time to assess these patterns can help you reclaim your time and redirect it toward what truly matters.

Practice the Tiny Rule

One of the principles I live by is something I call the Tiny Rule. Before making any new financial or life decision, I pause and ask myself, Does this support one of my fulfillment pillars? It's a small question, but it creates powerful alignment. Over time, I've found that asking it consistently keeps me centered on what truly matters and helps me make decisions that reflect the life I am building.

Chapter Summary

When I think about financial independence now, I do not see it as a finish line but as a framework for building a life that feels whole. For years, I chased numbers, titles, and milestones, believing that once I reached them, peace would follow. But I have learned that without fulfillment, even success can start to feel incomplete. Fulfillment transforms FIRE from a race to a number into a compass that guides your life.

Fulfillment gives money its meaning. It turns financial freedom into an opportunity to build a life rooted in purpose, growth, contribution, and connection. Fulfillment is personal and unique: what ignites one person may not move another. That's the beauty of it. Those four dimensions are guided decisions I have made since I began redefining what true wealth looks like.

And yet, staying aligned with what truly matters is not always easy. The distractions are real: the allure of shiny objects, the trap of comparison, and the grind of overwork can rob us of the very joy we seek. I have faced them too. What will keep you grounded is remembering that fulfillment is not a one-time achievement; it is something you return to, again and again, as your seasons and priorities shift.

When you know what you value, your choices begin to feel lighter. You spend differently. You plan differently. You even rest differently. The decisions about where your money goes start to reflect the kind of life you want to live. Fulfillment must be designed intentionally, choice by choice, day by day.

Your blueprint matters. By naming your non-negotiables, creating a Fulfillment Fund, and aligning your time with what matters most, you design a life that honors both your wealth and your wholeness. Financial independence was never meant to pull you away from working; it is meant to bring you closer to work that feels meaningful and aligned with your purpose.

Build intentionally, give generously, and let your wealth reflect what truly matters. Money is not the trophy but the tool that shapes a life rich in meaning, experiences, and legacy. Plant your resources as seeds of fulfillment and watch them grow into a harvest of joy and impact.

Wealth and Wisdom Declaration

Be transformed by the renewing of your mind, that you may prove what is that good, acceptable, and perfect will of God.

I boldly declare:

My wealth is not my identity; my wealth is an instrument of influence.

Money does not define me; meaning refines me.

I affirm that I am created by God to live a life of divine purpose, and my finances serve that calling.

I declare that money is my servant, not my master.

It moves at my instruction to fund what matters most; faith, family, freedom, and fulfillment.

I decree that every dollar in my hand becomes a seed of impact, birthing transformation in lives and generations.

I sow my resources into fertile fields of legacy, where miracles multiply, and blessings abound.

I confess that I refuse to chase money for its own sake.

I pursue meaning, mastery, and mission and wealth follows me by covenant.

I am no longer hustling for validation; I am building from revelation.

I affirm that I measure wealth not by accumulation, but by alignment; by joy, growth, contribution, and connection.

My prosperity is peace-filled; my abundance is anchored in gratitude.

I decree that I invest in experiences that stretch me, relationships that strengthen me, and impact that outlives me.

My name is associated with wisdom, generosity, legacy, and global transformation.

I declare that my daily decisions mirror my divine values.

I refuse to waste energy, time, or money on what does not serve my calling.

I am intentional with my stewardship, consistent in my strategy, and confident in my source.

I declare that my financial independence is not a trophy of toil but a harvest of peace, joy, and significance.

I am a wise gardener of resources; what I plant with intention flourishes into legacy.

I decree that my thoughts are wealthy, my words are wise, and my walk is worthy of divine prosperity.

Every limitation breaks before the force of renewed vision.

Every scarcity mindset bows to the abundance of my God.

I am FIRE'D Up to achieve financial freedom and purpose, to live richly in peace and passion, and to leave an imprint that outlives me.

My life is proof that wisdom creates wealth, and wealth fulfills purpose.

I am not striving; I am stewarding.

I am not chasing; I am choosing.

I am not surviving; I am soaring.

I reign in wisdom, walk in abundance, and rest in grace.

This is the mindset of a Millionaire Wo(man), rooted in purpose, crowned with peace, and overflowing with prosperity. Amen.

PART II

— THE FIRE'D UP ACCELERATOR SYSTEM™

Chapter
Four

INCOME DIVERSIFICATION (MAKE MONEY)

"A single paycheck is like standing on one leg, you can balance for a while, but one push can knock you over."

— Omolola Oyewumi

Most professionals were raised to believe that a steady paycheck equals security. Get a good job, work hard, and your income will always be there. But let's be honest: a paycheck is only as steady as the company, the boss, or the economy that funds it. And when that one stream stops, everything stops with it.

Depending on a single paycheck is like balancing on a tightrope without a safety net. It works, until it does not. A sudden reorganization, a market downturn, an unexpected illness, or even office politics can erase the income that supports your mortgage, your children's school fees, your groceries, and your dreams. That is not security but exposure. It's exposure because your stability depends on factors you cannot always control. Company budgets, leadership changes, or broader economic shifts can all impact your income overnight. Depending on one stream limits your ability to adjust when things change.

Now imagine standing on a platform supported by several beams instead of one. If one weakens, the others hold you steady. That's how income diversification works. When your income comes from different places, you don't live with the same fear or anxiety of losing your footing. There's reassurance in knowing that if one stream slows down, others can keep you supported. Income diversification moves your finances from fragility to being fortified.

When your income flows from more than one stream, you create space to make decisions from a place of confidence instead of fear. You stop asking, "What happens if I lose my job?" and start asking, "Where do I want my income to grow next?"

Research shows that 65% of millionaires have at least three streams of income. They don't leave their futures in the hands of a single paycheck, and neither should you. Income diversification is living securely, scaling faster, and creating freedom sooner. It strengthens your financial footing so one setback does not derail everything you've worked for. With multiple income streams, you are able to make decisions from a place of stability, take advantage of new opportunities, and build a future that gives you room to breathe and grow.

What the Numbers Reveal

Relying on a single paycheck is one of the riskiest financial positions you can be in. One decision whether a layoff, automation, or a health setback can erase it overnight. McKinsey estimates that by 2030, up to 25% of jobs may be displaced by automation.

Multiple income streams create options that produce courage. With alternatives in place, you no longer negotiate from fear. You can walk away from underpayment, toxic roles, or corporate politics with confidence.

Unlike salaries, which typically grow at a slow and predictable rate of about 3 to 5 percent each year, assets, investments, and small businesses build momentum through compounding. The money you put in begins to work for you, helping you pay debt faster, invest more consistently, and move closer to financial independence. Even an extra $500 or $1,000 a month can make a noticeable difference, shaving years off your timeline and moving your FIRE target years closer.

History proves it, too, during the 2020 pandemic, households with diversified income through rentals, digital products, or investments fared far better than those tied to a single paycheck. Diversification makes you resilient, even anti-fragile. Even when uncertainty rises, your finances remain stable because no single setback can undo all your progress.

But this goes beyond just money. Each new stream buys back time and gives you more control over your time, energy, and choices. It allows you to prioritize family, health, or purpose-driven projects while knowing your finances can support the life you are building. As Warren Buffett put it, "If you don't find a way to make money while you sleep, you will work until you die."

The future of work is already shifting. With AI, automation, remote economies, and portfolio careers becoming the norm, those who diversify now will be positioned to thrive while others scramble to adapt.

Accelerated Entrepreneurship

Entrepreneurship is one of the most powerful ways to accelerate both wealth and freedom. Salaries grow in small, predictable increments, but businesses have the potential to multiply. A job can provide stability, but entrepreneurship gives you the room to create and expand your income in ways most employers wouldn't permit.

I've seen what entrepreneurship can do, not just in others' lives, but in my own. My entrepreneurial spark started early. At 8 years, I started selling small goods to meet my own needs. At the time, it felt practical rather than visionary. But looking back, that was where I first learned that I could create opportunities rather than wait for them.

As my professional life developed, that spark grew with me. It turned into coaching, speaking, consulting, and writing avenues that helped me build income streams beyond my paycheck. Each time I built something outside my paycheck, I proved to myself that my earning power was not limited to corporate promotions or HR systems. That freedom became the engine of my FIRE'D UP journey.

The U.S. Lens: Structuring for Scale

In the U.S., entrepreneurship holds enormous potential, but only when it is built with structure and intention. The reason many side ventures stay small is that, too often, they're treated like hobbies rather than real businesses. Too many professionals view their business as just a side hustle meant to gain extra cash. Entrepreneurship should be a way to take ownership of your earning power. I learned early on that a great idea needs discipline, planning, and consistency to grow. If you want to experience acceleration, you must build for scale.

Once your side venture begins to grow, the goal is to build something that lasts. These steps will help you create a business that can scale, support your goals, and give you lasting freedom.

1. *Form the Right Entity*

Scaling your business starts with forming the proper legal structure. For many, that begins with an LLC (Limited Liability Company). It's simple to set up and separates your personal and business finances, protecting your personal assets and helping you appear more professional to clients and banks.

As your business grows, consider working with a CPA (Certified Public Accountant), a licensed financial professional who helps with taxes and business planning. A CPA can advise whether switching your LLC to an S-Corp makes sense. An S-Corp is not a new company type but a tax classification that can reduce self-employment taxes by allowing you to pay yourself partly as a salary and partly as profit.

2. *Separate Your Finances Early*

Open a business account and credit card. Track your numbers with financial tools like QuickBooks or Wave. Sometimes the best place to begin is with what ss already in front of you not with fancy software. Your bank and credit card statements can give you valuable insight into your spending patterns. Separating your finances makes tax season simpler, but more importantly, it creates the

financial foundation upon which your business can grow and stand strong.

3. *Think Like a Business Owner, not a Freelancer*

Don't trade hours for dollars; charge for the value you deliver. Clients recognize and pay for results that make a difference, not just the time it takes to produce them. To do that well, build repeatable systems that help you work efficiently: templates, onboarding flows, and automated emails that create consistency and free up your time for more meaningful work.

4. *Build a Tax and Retirement Strategy*

You need a tax strategy, not just a tax filing. A good CPA can help you plan, not just report what's already happened. Look into options that help you keep more of what you earn while saving for the future. This is the foundation of FIRE.

For example, a SEP IRA or Solo 401(k) allows self-employed individuals to contribute toward retirement while reducing taxable income. Some professionals also explore indexed universal life insurance (IULs) or annuities, which combine protection with long-term growth potential. These tools might sound complex, but they are simply ways to make your money work smarter, letting you reduce taxes and build long-term wealth simultaneously.

5. *Reinvest for Growth*

Finally, reinvest in growth. The temptation is to consume every profit, especially when the rewards of your hard work start to show. But true acceleration comes when you put some of that money back into your business. That might mean investing in better tools, stronger marketing, hiring a virtual assistant, or bringing on support so you can focus on higher-value work.

Reinvestment is what transforms a side hustle into a

sustainable business. Each time you pour resources back into growth, you strengthen your foundation and expand your capacity to earn more over time.

The Global Lens: Universal Entrepreneurship Principles

While the U.S. offers unique tax and structural advantages, the spirit of Accelerated Entrepreneurship applies everywhere. Whether you're in Canada, India, Nigeria, or Australia, the principles are the same.

1. **Start with what you have.** Your skills, your network, your environment, don't wait for the perfect business idea. Solve the problem already in front of you.

2. **Price with confidence.** Underpricing is universal. Wherever you live, your knowledge and creativity have value. Stop charging for survival, charge for transformation.

3. **Leverage technology.** The internet has flattened the world. From Lagos to London, digital products, e-commerce, and online coaching can reach global markets.

3. **Reinvest, don't extract.** Too many businesses plateau because profits are consumed too early. Growth happens when you put money back into systems, training, or expansion.

4. **Adapt to local ecosystems.** Maybe your country doesn't have LLCs or S-Corps, but most have small-business registrations, cooperatives, or even informal structures that provide legitimacy and separate personal from

business finances.

The truth is, opportunity looks different in every corner of the world. In India, a young professional who began teaching coding online on weekends turned her side hustle into a thriving ed-tech company serving students across Asia. In Nigeria, a mid-career accountant started a small financial literacy podcast that eventually grew into workshops and corporate training contracts. These stories may come from different markets, but they reveal the same principle, entrepreneurship accelerates freedom wherever it is practiced with intention.

Whether you're working within formal structures or building from an informal economy, the foundation is the same: solve a problem, stay consistent, and let your effort multiply over time.

The FIRE'd UP Stream Map

Financial independence accelerates when you move beyond one paycheck and intentionally design streams that complement and compound each other. The FIRE'D UP Stream Map lays out four wealth-building categories:

1. Skills-to-Cash (Active) – speed: immediate cash flow.

2. Digital Assets (Semi-Active Streams) – scalability: work once, earn repeatedly.

3. Asset-Backed Streams (Passive Income) – stability: long-term recurring income.

4. Compounding Streams (Financial Instruments) – momentum: wealth that multiplies itself.

Skills-to-Cash (Active Streams)

The quickest way to diversify your income is not by chasing more certifications, degrees, or new industries. It starts with what you already know. Skills-to-Cash is about turning your current skills into income streams that work for you right now, not years from now.

Think about it: the skills you use every day; problem-solving, managing projects, leading people, developing strategies, you do not have to stay locked inside your job. A project manager can help small businesses stay organized. A marketing professional can guide entrepreneurs through their first campaign. A financial analyst can consult for organizations that need short-term support. The very skills that earn you a paycheck can also earn you flexible, client-driven cash flow.

It also goes beyond your profession. If you've learned to navigate something challenging or built a system that works, there's someone who can benefit from that knowledge.

• Coaching, teaching, or mentoring others in career transitions, personal finance, wellness, or leadership can all become meaningful extensions of what you've lived and learned.

• People will pay for guidance in career transitions,

leadership, wellness, or money management.

• Education is another evergreen path: tutoring STEM students, teaching languages, or helping others ace standardized tests.

• The creative economy opens even more doors than most people realize. Designers, writers, photographers, and editors are helping businesses tell their stories in ways that connect with people.

• Those who are comfortable on a mic, or a stage find new audiences through speaking, whether in corporate boardrooms, conferences, workshops, or virtual summits.

• Even lifestyle and technical skills can open new opportunities. Fitness coaching, personal styling, home repair, or healthcare consulting may seem ordinary, but they each meet real needs.

When you share what you know with intention, those everyday abilities can grow into something meaningful and profitable.

"Almost any skill can become a stream of income when packaged with intention."

What makes Skills-to-Cash unbeatable is its speed. It creates immediate momentum, giving you cash to reinvest into longer-term wealth streams. Start here, and you'll never look at your skills the same way again. Unlike investing in real estate or building a startup, there's no need for massive capital or years of setup. You can start where you are, with what you know, and begin earning in days, not decades.

Digital Assets (Semi-Active Streams)

Digital assets are the bridge between active and passive income. They take effort to create in the beginning whether you are recording, designing, or building but once they are created, they can keep generating income long after the initial work is done. It's one of the simplest ways to make your time stretch further.

You don't need a massive following or a big platform to begin. Sometimes it is as simple as sharing what you already know. That could look like a short course that helps others avoid mistakes you have learned from, a digital toolkit that saves people time, or a resource that makes a process easier. These small, practical ideas can grow into a source of consistent income.

Digital assets can take many forms. Writers and creators build paid newsletters or online communities. Photographers and musicians license their work, so it continues to earn long after it's shared. Others create e-books, journals, or templates that quietly find their way into thousands of hands without requiring extra hours each week.

The beauty of digital assets lies in their scalability and their ability to free up your time. Once they're built, whether ten people buy or ten thousand, your effort stays the same. For busy professionals, this approach allows you to build an additional stream of income without sacrificing more time each week.

Digital Assets Examples

- Courses & Education Products: online courses, workshops, evergreen webinars.

- Digital Products & Tools: templates, planners, spreadsheets, apps, plug-ins.

- Content & Media: paid newsletters, membership communities, stock content licensing.

- Publishing: e-books, guides, journals, print-on-demand products.

- Creative Digital Works: artwork, NFTs, music, or video libraries.

Digital assets give you scale. Build once, and your work keeps working, even while you sleep.

Asset-Backed Streams (Passive Income)

Asset-backed streams use your money, property, or intellectual property to create recurring income. They require capital, planning, or ownership upfront, but once in motion, they can create cash flow that doesn't depend on your daily effort.

Real estate has long been the foundation for this kind of

wealth building through long-term rentals, short-term stays on Airbnb, or even passive investments in real estate funds (REITs). But assets go far beyond property. A car sitting idle can be rented out. Equipment can be leased. Extra storage space can bring in monthly income. Even vending machines and ATMs can quietly generate returns in the background.

For those who create, intellectual property is just as powerful. Royalties from books, music, digital tools, or frameworks can become a steady income stream that grows as your work reaches more people.

The common thread in all these examples is leverage. You are allowing your resources; financial, physical, or creative to keep working for you, even when you are not. These streams add stability to your financial foundation and help protect your income when life or the economy shifts unexpectedly.

Asset-Backed Streams Examples

- Real Estate: rentals (long-term, short-term, house-hacking), REITs, crowdfunding.

- Tangible Assets: vehicles, equipment, storage, vending machines, ATMs.

- Land & Property Use: leasing for farming, parking, or billboards.

- Royalties & Licensing: books, music, intellectual

property.

Asset-backed streams add stability. They build resilience into your financial house by creating income that endures.

Compounding Streams: (Financial Instruments)

Compounding is the quiet multiplier of wealth. – Omolola Oyewumi

While Skills-to-Cash creates speed, Digital Assets add scale, and Asset-Backed Streams bring stability, Compounding Streams are what turn today's savings into tomorrow's independence.

For most professionals, the starting point is simple. Broad-market index funds and dividend ETFs offer steady, diversified growth at relatively low cost. Retirement accounts like 401(k)s, IRAs, and Roth IRAs can take that even further by adding tax advantages and employer matches. Low-risk options such as high-yield savings accounts or bond ladders allow your short-term cash to keep earning in the background.

As your confidence grows, you will discover there are more advanced ways to build on that foundation. Cash value life insurance, dividend reinvestment plans (DRIPs), robo-advisors, and real estate funds (REITs) each combine automation and protection with long-term growth. For those comfortable with a bit of risk, crypto staking and other digital yield accounts can add another layer of opportunity—though always as a small, balanced fraction of the whole.

The principle stays the same: start early, stay consistent, and let time do the heavy lifting. Compounding rewards patience. Over time, it turns ordinary discipline into extraordinary progress.

Compounding Streams Examples

- Market Growth Engines: index funds, dividend ETFs, robo-advisors.

- Tax-Advantaged Accounts: 401(k), IRA, Roth IRA, HSAs.

- Income & Protection Vehicles: cash value life insurance, DRIPs, REITs.

- Safe Growth Options: bond ladders, high-yield savings acc ounts.

- Speculative Plays (small allocation): crypto staking, alternative digital yield.

The following instruments offer practical ways to put your money to work, each with unique strengths. Choose the ones that align with your goals and focus on applying them consistently.

Practical ways to put your money to work

No	Instrument	Risk Level	Liquidity	Minimum Investment	Time Horizon
01	Broad-Market Index Funds & Dividend ETFs	Moderate	High	$50/month	Long-term (10+ yrs)
02	Bond Ladders & Treasury Bills	Low	Low–Moderate	Varies	Short–Medium (1–10 yrs)
03	High-Yield Savings Accounts (HYSAs)	Very Low	High	None	Short-term (0–3 yrs)
04	Retirement Accounts (401k, IRA, Roth, Solo 401k)	Moderate	Low	Varies	Long-term (10+ yrs)
05	Cash Value Life Insurance (IULs & Whole Life)	Moderate–High	Low	Policy-dependent	Long-term (15+ yrs)
06	DRIPs (Dividend Reinvestment Plans)	Moderate	High	$10+	Long-term (10+ yrs)
07	Robo-Advisors (Automated Investing)	Moderate	High	$1+	Long-term (10+ yrs)
08	Real Estate Crowdfunding Platforms	Moderate–High	Low	$500–$1000	Medium–Long (5–15 yrs)
09	Health Savings Accounts (HSAs)	Low–Moderate	Moderate	Varies	Long-term (10+ yrs)
10	Peer-to-Peer Lending & Private Credit	High	Low	$25+	Medium-term (3–7 yrs)
11	REIT ETFs (Real Estate Investment Trust Funds)	Moderate	High	$50+	Medium–Long (5–15 yrs)
12	ESG & Impact Investing Funds	Moderate	High	$50+	Long-term (10+ yrs)
13	Precious Metal ETFs & Vaulted Savings	Moderate	High	$50+	Medium–Long (5–15 yrs)
14	Crypto Staking & Digital Yield Accounts	Very High	Low–Moderate	Varies	Speculative / Long-term

FIRE'D UP Insight

A modest $200 a month invested in a simple index fund can grow into more than $500,000 over 30 years at an 8% return. That's the quiet power of compounding. Time and consistency turn small steps into extraordinary freedom.

When combined, the four lanes of the FIRE'D UP Stream Map™ form what I call the Rule of Three Portfolio™—a framework for accelerating financial independence without relying on a single narrow path. You don't need all four at once; start with three and expand as your confidence grows.

For many immigrant professionals, the journey begins with what feels most accessible: high-yield savings accounts, REIT ETFs, simple robo-advisors, or crowdfunding platforms that accept an ITIN. Over time, as opportunities expand, you can layer in retirement accounts, HSAs, and tools like IULs.

What matters most isn't how complex your portfolio looks, but that it works for your life and goals. Each stream you add strengthens your foundation and builds a truly diversified engine for wealth that works across borders and across time.

Action Steps

FIRE'D UP Streams Map Framework

The FIRE'D UP Stream Map keeps income diversification simple, which is how to create more income, diversify income, earn beyond one paycheck and fast track financial independence. Choose three streams, build them consistently for one year, and let compounding multiply the results.

Step 1: Map Your Three Streams

Select one stream from each lane:

- Active (Skills-to-Cash): consulting, freelancing, or coaching that pays immediately. Clarify your model in one sentence: I help [who] achieve [result] through [method]. Simplicity sells.

- Semi-Active (Digital/Passive): a course, royalty, or rental income that pays beyond the first effort. Price by transformation, not hours. People invest in results.

- Compounding (Wealth Instruments): an index fund, retirement account, HSA (Health Savings Account), REIT (Real Estate Investment Trust Exchange-Traded Fund), ETF or IUL (Indexed Universal Life Insurance).

Step 2: Commit to 12 Months

Treat this as a one-year experiment. Focus your energy on three streams, not ten. When you give consistent attention to these three ideas, they grow faster and stronger.

Remember, the goal is progress, not perfection.

Step 3: Test in the First 30 Days

Launch something tangible quickly: sign your first client, publish the first module, or open your brokerage account. Small starts build confidence and evidence.

Step 4: Track and Reinvest

Set aside time each month to review your results. See what's working and what is not. Then, reinvest your earnings intentionally:

- 20–30% into better tools or resources

- 10–15% into learning, mentorship, or skill-building

- The rest into compounding streams that grow wealth long-term.

This rhythm keeps your money moving toward growth rather than getting stuck in consumption.

Step 5: Review Quarterly

Every 90 days, take a step back and evaluate your progress. Double down on what is gaining traction, pause what drains your time or energy, and refine your systems. This is where your side streams begin to mature into structured, repeatable income.

Step 6: Expand Over Time

The goal is balance, not busyness. Start with three. Grow

to five. At maturity, seven streams may be optimal. Most millionaires build freedom this way, not with dozens, but with focus.

By working this FIRE'D UP Streams Map, you move beyond the fragility of one paycheck. You design an income ecosystem that secures today, accelerates tomorrow, and funds freedom on your terms.

Chapter Summary

One decision or one downturn can erase 100% of your income. True financial resilience comes from diversification. This is the income engine, Money-making plan and stream strategy for FIRE acceleration.

Start with three streams one Active, one Semi-Active or Passive and one Compounding and build them intentionally for 12 months. Track your progress, reinvest your gains, and expand only once your foundation feels steady.

This rhythm keeps your focus sharp and your momentum consistent. Build slowly, intentionally, and with the confidence that each stream is moving you closer to freedom.

By building 3–7 resilient streams of income, you are no longer at the mercy of a paycheck you are the architect of your financial freedom.

Wealth and Wisdom Declaration

With discipline, wisdom, and faith, you are not limited to one paycheck, you are building an ecosystem of income that secures your freedom and fuels your purpose.

I boldly declare:

I am a wealth builder and a steward of divine creativity.

My gifts, skills, and ideas are seeds of wealth God has planted within me.

I speak life over my abilities, and I command them to multiply into streams of abundance.

I decree that I am not limited to one paycheck or one path.

I refuse the fragility of financial dependence.

The Lord is my Source, and He provides rivers in the desert and opportunities in unexpected places.

I affirm that every talent within me is a channel of impact, income, and freedom.

Nothing in my life is wasted; even my past experiences are capital for my future prosperity.

I walk boldly in divine innovation and creativity. My mind is a treasury of solutions.

I confess that I reject financial fragility and embrace financial resilience.

I am a wise architect of multiple income streams, each one anchored in purpose and strategy.

I build, I invest, I multiply, and I expand under divine instruction.

I declare that my work produces overflow, and my ideas yield abundance.

I do not hustle in fear; I create from faith.

My hands are blessed to produce profit, and my thoughts are anointed to create systems of sustainability.

I decree that I build streams that flow in harmony; active, passive, and compounding.

My Skills-to-Cash streams release quick wins.

My Digital Assets build leverage.

My Asset-Backed Streams create stability.

My Compounding Streams multiply legacy.

These rivers converge to fund freedom, fuel purpose, and fortify generations.

I affirm that my money works for me while I work for God.

My labor is not in vain; my harvest is generational.

I am disciplined, wise, and consistent in building wealth that aligns with my values and reflects heaven's excellence.

I confess that I do not chase money, I channel it.

I direct every resource toward impact, fulfillment, and legacy.

My financial ecosystem is divinely designed ordered, organized, and overflowing.

I decree that I walk in divine abundance.

My income ecosystem is secure, expanding, and anchored in God's promise of prosperity.

I am surrounded by streams that do not dry up, ideas that never expire, and opportunities that continually emerge.

I live under open heavens.

I multiply without measure.

I prosper without pressure.

I build wealth that serves purpose, blesses generations, and glorifies God. Amen.

Chapter
Five

MONEY MASTERY SYSTEMS (MANAGE MONEY)

From Money Stress to Money Mastery

Money can serve you faithfully or rule you harshly. Without a plan, good intentions collapse under the weight of emergencies and impulse. You can earn six figures and still feel broke if your money has no clear path. There was a time when my paycheck looked impressive on paper, yet I still felt the constant anxiety of "not enough." It was not until I began building systems, guardrails that worked even when I was tired, distracted, or overwhelmed, that I finally moved from money stress to money mastery.

The National Endowment for Financial Education reports that only 40% of U.S. households use a budget consistently. Yet those who do are far more likely to save, invest, and build wealth. In fact, the Consumer Financial Protection Bureau found that households with even a basic financial plan are three times as likely to reach financial goals. In other words, financial freedom is not about willpower but systems.

And the good news? Money mastery does not have to be complicated. Many people avoid financial planning because they picture spreadsheets, advanced math, or a high-level finance degree. In reality, true mastery looks remarkably simple: understanding what's coming in and what's going out. That awareness serves as the foundation for every wealth decision. From there, it's about intent, managing debt so it stops stealing your future, automating essentials so money grows without daily effort, and letting your income multiply on autopilot.

When you put these rhythms in place, everything changes. You stop asking, "Where did my money go?" and start asking, "Where is my money taking me?" You stop living at the mercy of bills, credit cards, and moods, and begin living from a place of design.

James Clear, author of Atomic Habits, once said: *"You don't rise to the level of your goals; you fall to the level of your systems."*

That wisdom has never been more accurate than in matters of money. Goals may inspire you, but systems are what sustain you. When your financial systems are strong, they free your mind to focus on building a life rooted in purpose and built for impact.

The purpose of this chapter is to show you how to build those systems one step at a time.

Cash Flow Is King

Every journey to financial independence begins with one simple, but powerful question: What is really happening with my money?

For most people, the honest answer is, "I don't know." Paychecks come in, bills go out, and somewhere in between, slips through their fingers. That gap: the mystery of "where did it all go?" is the silent killer of wealth.

Cash flow is the foundation of money mastery. If income diversification is the engine that drives FIRE, then cash flow is the steering wheel. Without it, you might be moving quickly, but not necessarily in the right direction. The formula is simple:

Cash Flow = Income – Expenses.

Positive cash flow: the surplus you keep after covering your needs is what builds wealth.

Negative cash flow: the shortfall when expenses outpace earnings is what buries people in debt. But simple doesn't mean easy. Many six-figure earners still struggle with negative or razor-thin cash flow because lifestyle inflation quietly absorbs every raise and bonus. A bigger paycheck often just means a bigger house, a newer car, and more subscriptions, the pressure stays the same, it just scales.

The Federal Reserve reports that nearly 40% of Americans would struggle to cover a $400 emergency and that includes many people earning solid incomes. Many professionals with substantial incomes still live one unexpected disruption away from financial chaos. The truth is that freedom begins with control. Until you understand and direct your cash flow, the future will always feel uncertain.

I learned this lesson during my own FIRE journey. Even with a comfortable income, I often felt stretched thin. Eventually, I started tracking every dollar not with an app, but with a simple notebook. That small step gave me a kind of clarity I hadn't felt before. I could finally see where the leaks were and how small changes created real progress over time. Later, I switched to apps and automation, but the core lesson stayed the same: when you manage what flows in and out, you take back control.

This is why I tell every client: don't guess your cash flow, know it. In fact, Intuit found that 65% of Americans don't know how much they spent last month. Most people don't need better math skills; they need better visibility into their finances.

Step 1: Awareness First

The first step in money mastery is radical awareness. Track every dollar that comes in and goes out for at least 30 days. Don't judge it, just observe it. Write it down in a notebook, use a spreadsheet, or try an app like YNAB (You Need a Budget), Mint, or Monarch Money.

Once you start tracking, two things happen:

• First, the fog begins to lift. You finally see the truth of your habits, not the version you have been assuming.

• Second, opportunities appear. You start to notice leaks didn't see before, subscriptions you don't use, dining out habits that quietly add up, or impulse purchases that eat into your long-term goals.

Awareness is the first domino in money mastery. Give yourself thirty honest days of observation, and you will be surprised by how much control you gain just from paying attention.

Step 2: Forecast, Don't Budget: The Expansive Mindset

Traditional budgeting certainly has its place, but let's be honest: for many professionals, it feels like punishment. Budgets often sound like, "Cut back. Live smaller." While discipline can be helpful, spending your whole financial life in restriction leaves little space for joy or growth.

My mentor, Loral Langemeier, author of Put More Cash in Your Pocket, taught me something simple but freeing: budgets focus on limits; forecasting focuses on growth. Forecasting changes the question from "What do I cut?" to:

• How can I earn what I need for the life I desire?

• What skills can I leverage to bring in more?

- What opportunities can I create that turn this expense into an investment rather than a burden?

The shift is subtle but transformational. Suddenly, money becomes a tool you command rather than a leash you are tethered to. You are not trimming life down to fit into a box but building the box bigger to fit the life you actually want.

Step 3: Buckets of Purpose

But when you give it direction, it grows and builds stability over time. Think of your cash flow as soldiers in your financial army: if they don't have clear orders, they wander aimlessly.

The best way to make your money work is to give every dollar a job. That's where "buckets" come in. Each one represents a category that supports your goals and reflects your values. Here are ten purposeful "buckets" where every dollar should be directed:

1. Living Costs: The essentials: rent/mortgage, food, utilities, transportation.

2. Freedom Fund: Savings and investments that accelerate your path to FIRE.

3. Debt Crusher: Allocations to aggressively pay down high-interest debt.

4. Joy Fund: Experiences, travel, and luxuries that remind you that life is for living now.

5. Protection: Insurance premiums, legal coverage, or extended warranties that shield your wealth.

6. Emergency Cushion: Contributions to your 3–6-month safety net for life's curveballs.

7. Growth & Learning: Courses, certifications, conferences, or coaching that expand your skills and earning power.

8. Generosity: Tithing, charitable giving, or community support aligned with your values.

9. Legacy Building: Saving toward education funds, intergenerational wealth accounts, or trusts.

10. Dream Projects: Seed money for business ventures, passion projects, or big future goals.

Start by naming your buckets and assigning each dollar a purpose. When you do, the fog around your finances starts to clear. You'll begin to see where your money is actually going and, more importantly, where you want it to take you.

Step 4: Wipe Out Debt with Precision

Debt is one of the heaviest weights you can carry on the road to financial independence. It slows your progress, clouds your vision, and makes freedom feel out of reach. Many professionals had said to me that they are awake at night, calculating bills in their heads, wondering if they will ever be free. That is the real cost of debt, not just the interest, but the mental and emotional toll it takes. The anxiety steals your peace and delays you from building the wealth you desire.

The most effective debt paydown strategies share one thing in common: clarity. You must know precisely what you owe, to whom, and at what interest rate. Without that clarity, every payment feels random, and your efforts feel ineffective. Once you have a clear picture, there are proven methods that make debt repayment strategic rather than stressful.

1. *Attack High-Interest Debt First*

Credit cards and payday loans often carry interest rates of over 20%. Left unchecked, they multiply faster than most investments ever could. The first order of business is to cut off this compounding enemy. Pour every extra dollar you can find into these balances, while paying minimums on everything else. Every payment is like reclaiming stolen ground and your peace of mind.

2. *The Avalanche Method*

This strategy focuses on math. List all your debts from highest to lowest interest rate and tackle them in that order. The avalanche method saves you the most money over time because you're dismantling the costliest liabilities first. One of my clients adopted this system after years of paying "whatever he could" each month. In just 16 months, he wiped out over $23,000 of consumer debt and freed up $700 a month that now goes straight into investments. That single shift shortened his path to financial independence by nearly a decade.

3. *The Snowball Method*

Some people are not motivated by math. If you are more motivated by momentum than numbers, this approach works wonders. The snowball method lines up debts from smallest to largest. You focus on the smallest debt first, then roll that payment into the next, and the next, until you are on a winning streak. Psychologically, this works wonders. Each quick win fuels your determination, and soon enough, you have a snowball effect of progress that feels unstoppable. Progress becomes visible, and that feeling of control returns. This is mostly and widely used by my clients.

4. *Use Debt Strategically*

Not all debt is destructive. A mortgage that builds equity, a student loan that expands earning potential, or a carefully structured business loan that funds growth, these can be assets if managed wisely. The key is to differentiate between debt that supports your future and debt that only drains it. Smart debt should always have a clear return on investment.

Emergency Fund: Your Financial Shock Absorber

An emergency fund is the unsung hero of money mastery. It does not make headlines and won't impress anyone at dinner parties, but it will save you when life throws a curveball. Unexpected expenses are not a matter of if, but a matter of when. A medical bill, a car repair, a sudden job loss, or even a leaking roof can unravel the best-laid financial plans and years of progress if you are not prepared. Without a safety net, those moments often push people right back into credit cards, loans, and cycles of debt. That is why having an emergency fund is a necessity.

Financial planners often recommend saving three to six months of living expenses, and there is a good reason for that. Studies from the Federal Reserve show that nearly 40% of Americans would struggle to cover a $400 emergency without borrowing. That statistic alone highlights the fragility of most households' finances. As the FIRE'D UP Queen, I would recommend 12 to 18 months of your living expenses. Look at what happened during Covid 19, how long did the pandemic lasted? Now, I've seen how this simple habit changes lives. Debt freedom without an emergency fund is like building a house without a foundation. It looks stable until the storms hit.

Here's how to start an emergency fund:

1. Begin with a starter fund of $1,000 - $3,000 as fast as you can, sell something, pause extras, put aside that tax refund or redirect a bonus.

2. Build steadily toward the three to six months cushion, automating transfers so it grows without effort.

3. Keep it liquid and accessible; a high-yield savings account (like CIT.com, Ally, or Marcus) helps it grow without risk.

It's important to remember that your emergency fund is assurance, not an investment. It's not meant to yield returns the way an investment account would. The goal of this fund is to fortify your finances and ensure they remain intact even when emergencies arise.

Automate and Accelerate

One of the most powerful turning points in my FIRE'D UP journey came the day I stopped trying to "remember" my money moves and started building systems to handle them for me. Up until then, I would make transfers when I had time, pay down debt when I felt motivated, and invest when I remembered. While emotions are unreliable, systems, on the other hand, keep their promises even on your busiest or most challenging days.

Automation takes the decision-making out of your hands and places it into a system that executes your priorities without you having to lift a finger. Instead of wondering, "Did I save this month?" or "Did I move that extra payment?" you begin to live with the confidence that it is already handled. It gives you back bandwidth to focus on the bigger picture to dream, create, and build the life you have been planning for.

Once your money is automated, something even more remarkable happens, it begins to multiply. Every automated transfer to savings strengthens your safety net. Every recurring investment into index funds or retirement accounts compounds in the background. Every scheduled extra loan payment shortens your debt horizon by years. And because these moves happen on autopilot, they are not dependent on your memory, mood, or willpower. They simply happen.

This is what mastery feels like; your money grows while you are working, resting, or even on vacation. Its why Albert Einstein called compound interest the "eighth wonder of the world." Also, John Bogle insisted that staying the course beats chasing the market. Thought leaders like Ramit Sethi teach automated investing as the foundation of effortless wealth building.

The math is undeniable: $1,000 invested every month for 20 years at 8% returns grows to nearly $600,000. The earlier you automate, the sooner time and compounding become your biggest allies. In my own life, that shift changed everything. I noticed I no longer needed to "feel" motivated or wait for the "right moment" to save or invest. The day after every payday, my accounts handled the work for me.

At first, the progress was almost invisible. The numbers moved slowly, almost unnoticeably, but they moved. Then one day, I looked at my accounts and realized how much ground I had covered without even thinking about it. That quiet acceleration, the kind you don't notice until one day your account looks different is the hallmark of autopilot wealth.

I realized financial growth doesn't need to feel dramatic to be effective. It just needs to be consistent. The goal is to make your money work harder than you do.

Action Steps:

Build Your Autopilot System

Money mastery flows from systems that carry the weight for you, even on the days you are busy, tired, or distracted. Think of this as your financial autopilot, where each dollar is given a job, and your goals are funded automatically. Here is how to set it up:

Secure Your Foundation

Start with safety. Build an Emergency Fund that covers three to six months of living expenses in a high yield savings account and automate monthly transfers until it is full. At the same time, set up automatic extra payments on high-interest debt. Whichever one is your preference; Avalanche or Snowball method, the key is to make progress automatic. When your system handles it, consistency becomes effortless.

Automate Wealth-Building

Consistency will always outperform intensity. Set up

recurring contributions to your retirement accounts; 401(k), Roth IRA, or HSA and automate monthly investments into diversified index funds or ETFs. This approach, called dollar-cost averaging, removes the guesswork and emotion from investing. Over time, those steady contributions compound into something meaningful. Treat it like a non-negotiable bill to your future self.

Automate Meaningful Living

Create a Fulfillment Fund for the things that make life rich like; travel, learning, creativity, and giving. Automate your generosity too, through recurring transfers to charities or causes that align with your values. When your giving is consistent, it becomes part of how you live, not just something you do when it's convenient.

Review & Forecast

Systems are not "set it and forget it" neither do they run themselves forever, but they should be set and refined over time. Check in quarterly to review your progress your net worth, debt reduction, and

fulfillment Fund growth. Once a year, you should rebalance your investments and adjust contributions as your income changes. Then look ahead. Forecast what's next and assign dollars to goals in advance.

As Loral Langemeier says in Put More Cash in Your Pocket:

"Forecasting turns money from a source of stress into a

tool for expansion."

When your financial life is automated, you no longer rely on memory or willpower to progress. You are letting structure do the work for you. That is how everyday professionals build extraordinary results. They are not hustling nonstop; instead, they create systems that keep moving even when life gets busy. Your autopilot system is proof that wealth requires you to use wisdom and stay consistent.

Chapter Summary

When your money runs on systems, a sense of steadiness begins to take root. You are no longer chasing bills or second-guessing where your money went. Instead, you can see your financial picture clearly and make choices with confidence. Money mastery is not about getting everything perfect or micromanaging every dollar; it is about building a framework that keeps working even when life feels unpredictable.

If you have ever opened your account and felt that familiar wave of frustration or confusion, you are not the only one. I've been there too, multiple times on this wealth building journey. What changed everything for me was having simple, reliable systems in place. The more structure I built, the less stress I carried.

Cash flow brings awareness and direction, debt management restores control, and automation keeps progress moving even when you are not watching. An emergency fund turns unexpected events into temporary setbacks rather than crises, and compounds reward your consistency, growing your wealth in the background.

If things still feel uncertain, don't rush the process. Real change happens gradually, through steady, repeatable actions. Each time you track your spending, make a payment, or adjust an automated transfer, you are strengthening your foundation and stepping toward financial freedom.

Momentum is the heartbeat of money mastery. Once your system is in motion, progress becomes more natural, and your future starts to take shape with more intention.

Wealth and Wisdom Declaration

Systems create stability. Automation builds acceleration. Momentum sustains mastery.

These declarations align your faith, habits, and mindset with the principles that accelerate financial independence.

I boldly declare:

Systems create stability, and discipline creates freedom.

Wealth is not built by accident but is built by design, through order, stewardship, and divine wisdom.

I am a wise architect of abundance, designing systems that multiply what I have and secure what I build.

I declare that God has given me supernatural wisdom to steward money with excellence.

My systems work in divine order and multiply my resources beyond logic.

My finances obey my strategy, and my strategy obeys divine instruction.

I affirm that I walk in clarity and confidence.

My cash flow is under my command; every dollar I earn carries a divine assignment.

Money does not drift aimlessly in my hands, it flows purposefully toward my God-given goals.

I decree that the hold of debt is broken over my life.

I owe no one anything but love.

I am accelerating into freedom with discipline, strategy, and joy.

My mindset is debt-free, my record is clean, and my heart is at peace.

I confess that I am faithful with little, and God is making me ruler over much.

I am not careless with my coins; I am conscious with my capital.

My finances are organized, protected, and fruitful.

My accounts are balanced, my records are accurate, and my plans are blessed.

I declare that automation works in my favor.

While I rest, my savings grow, my investments compound, and my future expands.

My systems are my servants, they work diligently even in my absence.

I affirm that my emergency fund is a shield of wisdom.

I will never be caught unprepared; divine provision covers every unexpected storm.

I live in readiness, not reaction. I plan with foresight, not fear.

I decree that money flows to me in alignment with purpose.

I master my money and money does not master me.

My budget is a blueprint, not a burden.

My spending serves my strategy, and my habits reflect my vision.

I declare peace over my household.

Financial stress gives way to divine order.

Chaos is replaced with abundance and calm.

Harmony fills my home because I have invited heaven into my systems.

I affirm that my financial order creates generational blessing.

My children and their children rise to enjoy the fruits of my discipline.

They inherit not only wealth but wisdom, not only money but mastery.

I decree that I live in abundance, not scarcity.

I partner with God to multiply resources and to walk in wealth with meaning, freedom, and fulfillment.

I forecast, I automate, I give, I grow, and I overflow.

My systems are anointed.

My accounts are abundant.

My future is fortified.

I am FIRE'D UP to manage, multiply, and master my money for purpose, peace, and prosperity. Amen.

Chapter
Six

WEALTH GROWTH & PROTECTION
(MULTIPLY & PROTECT MONEY)

I want you to read this chapter as if we are sitting across the table, two professionals with full calendars and big goals. You already know how to earn. The real question is how to make your money move with the same purpose and consistency that you do, how to build wealth that grows, stays protected, and buys back your time without shrinking your life to fit a smaller budget.

Remember how I mentioned that most people even high earners would struggle to cover a small emergency in cash? That reality doesn't come from a lack of effort. Often it happens when money flows in but never gets directed with intention. This chapter is about changing that pattern for good.

That is where the Triple Shield Framework™ comes in, a

method that helps your income grow with purpose, stay protected from setbacks, and preserve more of what it earns. The goal is expansion, not restriction. It is about putting your dollars to work, building assets that pay you, and letting your skills compound into ownership. As Loral reminds us, the aim is not endless saving or self-denial but creating more cash through smarter systems.

Let's begin with the first layer: how to make your money multiply on its own. A modest habit, like investing $500 a month into a broad index fund, can grow to more than $745,000 over 30 years at an 8% return. Most of that isn't from what you contributed; it's from what is compounding. Robert Kiyosaki said it best: the wealthy build machines, not just paychecks.

Professionals face liability, market swings, and unexpected health events. Nearly 70% of Americans over 65 will need some form of long-term care, a cost that can quietly erode decades of savings. Protection ensures that progress lasts, keeping your options open no matter what comes.

Then there's the silent drain: taxes. State and local taxes take about 11% of income before federal taxes even begin. For many households, taxes are their largest recurring expense. Every dollar you legally keep is another that keeps growing. Wallace D. Wattles called this "efficient action", doing what works and capturing the benefit. We will apply that same principle to tax planning.

By the end, you'll have a clear blueprint for multiplying

what you earn and defending what you build, growth that runs automatically, protection that turns setbacks into pauses instead of spirals, and tax efficiency designed for builders.

This is wealth, the expansive way: turning skills into assets, assets into cash flow, and cash flow into freedom. The framework ahead is strong enough to carry you through bull markets, bear markets, and everything in between. As Wattles wrote, "By thought, the thing you want is brought to you; by action you receive it." This chapter is where the action begins.

The Triple Shield Framework

In my years of helping professionals rethink wealth, I have learned that most people don't fall short because they lack intelligence or discipline. The problem is usually direction. Many work hard and earn well but build without a clear blueprint. The Triple Shield Framework™ offers that structure. This teaches you how wealth works, how wealth is built safely, how to avoid financial disaster and how to set up a stable structure before they earn more.

It gives your money form, focus, and staying power. This framework rests on three essential shields:

1. Growth Vehicles: strategies and assets that multiply wealth through compounding and momentum.

2. Protection Vehicles: safeguards that preserve progress when life delivers the unexpected.

3. Tax Efficiency: tools and structures that help you keep more of what you earn, so it continues to compound.

Each shield reinforces the others. Growth accelerates your journey. Protection ensures that progress endures. Tax efficiency prevents leaks that slow you down. Together, they form a living system one that does not just build wealth but sustains it through every season of life and work.

When I began applying this framework myself, I noticed how quickly financial calm replaced financial chaos. I was building on purpose. That's the shift I want for you too, less strain, more strategy. The Triple Shield Framework is about control, so your money finally supports the life you are designing instead of dictating it.

Growth Vehicles: Compounding as Your Wealth Engine

Every professional knows the discipline of showing up, putting in the hours, and climbing the ladder. But real wealth begins when your money starts doing that work with you. That is where growth vehicles come in, systems that help your wealth multiply through compounding and consistent progress.

Compounding works because it honors a few simple truths:

- *Time is your greatest multiplier.* The earlier you start, the stronger the exponential effect. A Fidelity study showed that a single $10,000 investment at age 25 can outgrow decades of larger contributions that begin later.

- **Consistency beats timing.** Automated contributions, month after month, outperform attempts to predict the market. Staying invested through the highs and lows allows compounding to do its best work.

- **Reinvestment accelerates results.** Dividends and interest may seem small but reinvesting them fuels future growth. Over 40% of stock market returns in the past half-century came from reinvested dividends.

- **Patience pays.** Compounding builds slowly at first, then rapidly. Charlie Munger once said, *"The big money is not in the buying or the selling, but in the waiting."* And this principle extends far beyond the stock market:

- **Dividend Reinvestment Plans (DRIPs):** Reinvesting dividends in ETFs or stocks builds a self-reinforcing loop of growth.

- **Debt Payoff:** Paying off high-interest debt can be the same as earning a guaranteed return. Eliminating an 18% credit card balance equals an 18% risk-free gain.

- **Real Estate Equity Loops:** Properties appreciate, equity builds, and refinancing allows you to reinvest in new assets, turning one property into many.

- **Cash Value Insurance:** Certain policies, like Indexed Universal Life, allow for tax-advantaged growth while you borrow against their value, letting your money compound uninterrupted.

The goal of these vehicles is to create steady motion, cycles that keep your money producing value over time. Wallace Wattles wrote in The Science of Getting Rich: "You must give every man more in use value than he gives you in cash value." Financially, that means positioning each dollar, so it gives back more than it costs to earn. The longer you keep this system running, the faster the wheel turns toward financial independence.

Protection Vehicles: Safeguarding Wealth

Earning and investing get the spotlight, but protection is what keeps everything together. It is the layer that keeps your wealth serving you, your family, and your goals, no matter what life throws at you. Growth helps you build wealth, but protection ensures you keep it.

Benjamin Franklin once said, "An ounce of prevention is worth a pound of cure."

Protection vehicles embody that wisdom. They do not restrict growth; they safeguard it. Wealthy families have long known that building wealth is only half the game; the other half is preserving it. Protection gives peace of mind that your work, your assets, and your legacy are secure against life's unpredictability.

Below are some protective vehicles to safeguard your wealth:

Insurance Shields: The First Line of Defense

Insurance often feels like an unnecessary expense until the day it saves you. For professionals, the right coverage is foundational:

- **Life Insurance:** Provides for dependents if income stops. Term life is straightforward and affordable, while Indexed Universal Life (IUL) can double as a tax-advantaged growth vehicle.

- **Disability Insurance:** One in four workers will face disability before retirement age. This ensures your income, the asset on which everything else depends, remains protected.

- **Umbrella Liability Insurance:** Extends beyond auto or home policies, covering lawsuits and high-liability risks that can target your assets and reputation.

- **Long-Term Care Insurance:** Nearly 70% of Americans over 65 will need some form of care, often costing $4,000–$9,000 per month. Coverage prevents these expenses from draining a lifetime of savings.

Insurance does not generate wealth, but it creates the space for everything else to keep compounding.

Legal Structures: Building the Walls

Wealthy families use the law as a shield, not as luck. The right legal structures bring clarity and confidence that your hard work won't be undone by risk or dispute:

- **LLCs (Limited Liability Companies):** Separate personal finances from business risks, shielding homes, savings, and retirement accounts from lawsuits.

- **Trusts:** Define how assets transfer, reduce probate costs, sometimes add tax advantages, and preserve your legacy for the next generation.

These tools are less about complexity and more about alignment. They ensure you have control and confidence that disputes or vulnerabilities won't consume your wealth.

Diversification & Liquidity: The Moats and Drawbridges

Balance protects wealth as much as insurance does. Diversification spreads risk, and liquidity buys time.

- **Diversification:** Allocates assets across industries, classes, and geographies. If one area struggles, others stabilize the portfolio.

- **Liquidity**: A resilience fund of 6–12 months of living expenses in a high-yield savings or money market fund. This prevents the forced selling of long-term investments during a crisis. Liquidity is your drawbridge it ensures access to resources when you need them most.

Tax Efficiency: Plugging the Wealth Leaks

You can earn more, save consistently, and invest wisely, but if taxes erode those gains, it can feel like running in place. Picture your finances as a bucket you are trying to fill. Every dollar you earn and invest adds more water, yet taxes create small holes that let it seep out just as quickly. The harder you pour, the more escapes through those leaks. The goal is not to earn more, it's to patch the holes so your effort actually builds up inside the bucket.

A thoughtful tax plan does precisely that. It keeps more of what you pour in, allowing your wealth to rise instead of drain away. "It is not the number of things you do, but the efficiency of each separate thing you do, that counts." The same principle applies here: make every move count.

Here are the most powerful strategies to protect your wealth through a thoughtful tax plan:

Choose the Right Accounts

The simplest way to boost efficiency is to use tax-advantaged accounts that let more money compound for your future.

- **W-2 Professionals:** Employer-sponsored accounts like 401(k)s or 403(b)s reduce taxable income today while investments grow tax-deferred. Employer matches are essentially free money. If available, Roth 401(k)s let you contribute after-tax and withdraw tax-free in retirement.

- **Entrepreneurs & Side-Hustlers:** Solo 401(k)s and SEP IRAs allow larger contributions, since you're both "employee" and "employer." In 2025, that can mean up to $69,000 (or $76,500 if over 50). HSAs offer a rare triple advantage, contributions reduce taxable income, growth is tax-free, and qualified withdrawals are tax-free.

Time Withdrawals Wisely

Tax planning is not only about how you save but also about when you spend. Timing can make a significant difference over a lifetime.

- **Roth Conversions:** Moving money from a traditional IRA to a Roth IRA during low-income years (like sabbaticals or early business years) means paying less tax now and avoiding it later.

- **Withdrawal Sequencing:** Drawing from taxable accounts first, then letting retirement accounts grow, often reduces required minimum distributions and smooths taxes over time.

- **Capital Gains Harvesting:** In lower-income years, you can sell appreciated assets, pay little or no tax, and reset your cost basis for future growth.

Leverage Real Estate

The tax code was written with property owners in mind, offering multiple advantages:

- **Depreciation:** Deduct part of a property's value each year, often sheltering rental income.

- **1031 Exchanges**: Defer capital gains by rolling proceeds from one property into another "like-kind" investment.

- **Cost Segregation:** Accelerate deductions by depreciating property components faster.

- **Refinancing to Unlock Equity:** Borrowing against appreciation doesn't trigger taxes, freeing capital to reinvest while properties continue to grow.

Give with Intention

Generosity can be one of the most fulfilling and effective tax strategies. When giving is structured well, it reduces taxes, strengthens causes you care about, and builds legacy.

- **Donor-Advised Funds (DAFs):** Deduct now, give later. Contributions reduce taxable income in high-earning years, while funds can grow before being granted to charities.

- **Charitable Remainder Trusts (CRTs):** Provide income during your lifetime, avoid immediate capital gains on appreciated assets, and leave the remainder to charity.

- **Appreciated Securities:** Donate stocks or funds directly to avoid capital gains and claim a deduction for the full value.

- **Global Equivalents:** Whether in the U.S., U.K., or elsewhere, most countries offer vehicles for tax-advantaged giving such as foundations, trusts, or donor accounts.

Use Business Structures to Your Advantage

Once you earn outside your paycheck through consulting, freelancing, or real estate, you step into the business arena. The right setup turns income into opportunity.

- **Sole Proprietorship:** Simple for small side hustles but offers no liability protection.

- **LLCs**: Separate personal assets from business risks, allow expense deductions, and provide flexible taxation.

- **S-Corps:** Let you split income between salary and dividends, reducing self-employment taxes once profits grow.

- **C-Corps:** Best for raising investment or reinvesting profits, though less common for small ventures.

Even W-2 professionals benefit once side income grows. Business structures reduce taxes, expand deductions, and increase contribution limits for retirement accounts.

The Philosophy of Tax Efficiency

Each of these strategies acts like a layer of protection. One layer lets your retirement savings grow untaxed. Another defers taxes on real estate. Another aligns wealth with your values through giving. Another channels business income through structures that maximize efficiency. These all creates a network that keeps your money compounding and aligned with your values.

Business Structures at a Glance

Structure	Best For	Tax Treatment	Pros	Cons
Sole Proprietorship	Sole hustlers just starting out (consulting, freelancing, small gigs).	Income flows directly to personal return, subject to self-employment tax.	Easy to set up, minimal cost, no paperwork.	No liability protection, all income taxed at self-employment rate.
LLC	Small businesses ($20k-$100k+), freelancers, real estate investors.	Pass-through taxation by default, can elect S-Corp status.	Liability protection, flexible, separates personal and business finances.	Annual fees and compliance vary by state.
S-Corp	Growing businesses ($50k-$1M+ net profit), consultants, agency owners.	Salary subject to payroll tax, remaining profits distributed as dividends.	Saves on self-employment tax, higher retirement contributions, liability protection.	More paperwork, payroll setup, IRS scrutiny on "reasonable salary."
C-Corp	Startups seeking investors, large-scale businesses, tech companies.	Double taxation: corporate profits taxed, then dividends taxed to shareholders.	Attractive for raising capital, no shareholder limits, reinvested profits taxed at 21%.	Complex compliance, double taxation unless profits reinvested.

If You are Outside the U.S.

While these structures are based on U.S. terminology, the same principles apply worldwide. In the U.K., you'll see Limited Companies (Ltd); in Canada, Corporations (Inc); in India, Private Limited Companies (Pvt Ltd); and in the UAE, Free Zone Entities.

Each system has its own rules and tax treatments, but the purpose is universal: to create a legal shield around your personal assets and give your income more flexibility.

Wherever you live, the guiding questions remain the same: How do I protect my personal wealth from business risks? How can I structure income so that it grows efficiently? The answers may look different by country, but the strategy of using structure to your advantage applies everywhere.

The FIRE'D UP Wealth-Growth Matrix

Beyond business setup, the next step is understanding how your money can grow and protect itself across different vehicles. The FIRE'D UP Wealth-Growth Matrix compares the most common options and how they perform in real life:

The FIRE'D UP Wealth-Growth Matrix

Vehicle	Growth Potential	Risk Level	Liquidity	Tax Efficiency	Protection Factor
Broad Market Index Funds (ETFs/Mutual Funds)	High (7-10% historical/average)	High (7-10% historical/average)	High (can sell quickly)	High (in retirement accounts 401k, IRA)	Moderate (diversified but exposed to downturns)
Dividend-Paying Stocks / DRIPs	Moderate-High (steady compounding)	Moderate-High (steady compounding)	High	Moderate (taxable dividends unless in Roth/IRA)	Moderate (income stream but market-dependent)
Bonds & Treasury Securities	Low-Moderate (2-5%)	Low-Moderate (2-5%)	High	Moderate (munis tax-advantaged)	High (government-backed, stable)
Real Estate (Direct Ownership)	High (appreciation + rental income)	High (appreciation + rental income)	Low (illiquid)	High (depreciation, write-offs, 1031 exchange)	High (hard asset, inflation hedge)
REITs & Real Estate ETFs	Moderate-High (dividends + appreciation)	Moderate-High (dividends + appreciation)	High (traded on exchanges)	Moderate	Moderate (sector diversification but market-linked)
Cash Value Life Insurance (IUL/Whole Life)	Moderate (4-7% long-term)	Moderate (4-7% long-term)	Low (loan access vs. surrender)	High (tax-deferred growth, tax-free loans)	Very High (death benefit + asset protection)
Precious Metals (Gold, Silver, etc.)	Low-Moderate (hedge, not growth)	Low-Moderate (hedge, not growth)	High (easily sold)	Low	High (inflation hedge, safe-haven asset)
Private Equity / Venture Capital	Very High (10-30% potential)	Very High (10-30% potential)	Very Low (long lock-ups)	Variable	Low (speculative, not protective)
Cryptocurrency / Digital Assets	Very High (20% + possible)	Very High (20% + possible)	High (but exchange risks exist)	Low	Low (speculative, not protective)
HSA (Health Savings Account)	Moderate-High (triple tax advantage)	Low	Moderate (for health expenses, penalties otherwise)	Very High (triple tax-free)	High (health-focused security)
Annuities (Fixed / Indexed)	Low-Moderate (steady but capped)	Low (guaranteed by insurer)	Low-Moderate (depends on terms)	High (tax-deferred until payout)	Very High (guaranteed lifetime income)

This matrix is not an invitation to pick everything. Choose wisely and with intention. Busy professionals do not need to chase every opportunity. Align each vehicle with your goals and timeline.

Early and mid-career readers may lean toward equities and select alternatives for higher growth over longer horizons.

Those nearing financial independence may favor real estate, quality bonds, and tax-advantaged accounts for income, stability, and preservation. The right blend balances progress with resilience.

How to Use the Matrix

- Growth Potential shows how fast wealth can multiply.

- Risk Level reflects exposure to market swings, defaults, or loss.

- Liquidity indicates how quickly you can access funds without penalties.

- Tax Efficiency measures how well the vehicle shields wealth from taxes.

- Protection Factor highlights the role each vehicle plays in safeguarding wealth.

Action Steps

- **Activate Your Growth Engine:** Put your wealth on autopilot. Set up an automatic contribution into a compounding vehicle like an index fund, retirement account, or DRIP. Start small if you must, but let consistency do the heavy lifting.

- **Strengthen Your Protection Shields:** Review your insurance coverage with fresh eyes. Do your life, disability, umbrella, and long-term care policies reflect your current reality? Update beneficiaries so your wealth transfers exactly as intended.

- **Plug the Tax Leaks:** Taxes silently erode wealth. Commit to maxing out at least one tax-advantaged account this year; whether a 401(k), Roth IRA, HSA, or Solo 401(k) if you're self-employed. If you're outside the U.S., identify the equivalent in your country and build the habit of contribution.

- **Design Your Real Estate Play:** If you already own property, explore strategies like depreciation or refinancing to advance your wealth plan. If you don't, research whether real estate fits your diversification strategy and timeline.

- **Protect Your Side Hustle:** If you're building income outside your 9–5, don't treat it casually. Open a separate account, track your expenses, and explore forming an LLC. Treat it like the business it has the potential to become.

- **_Give with Strategy and Intention:_** Wealth has meaning when it flows outward. Choose one course you care about and align your giving with your wealth plan, whether through a Donor-Advised Fund, appreciated assets, or structured charitable contributions.

- **_Build Your Resilience Fund:_** Storms will come. Safeguard 6–12 months of living expenses in a liquid account so downturns never force you into desperate decisions.

- **_Schedule Your Strategy Session:_** Do not do it alone. Book time with a financial planner, tax advisor, or attorney to stress-test your plan. Guidance from experts is not an expense, it is an accelerant.

Chapter Summary

Wealth growth and protection are not competing priorities but companions on the same journey. Growth fuels your financial independence, while protection ensures it lasts. Tax efficiency acts as the hidden accelerator, allowing every dollar to operate at full strength.

The Triple Shield Framework creates a fortress around your wealth: growth vehicles to expand it, protection vehicles to defend it, and tax strategies to keep it compounding without waste.

With the FIRE'D UP Wealth Growth Matrix, you now hold both the blueprint and the map. It shows how different vehicles perform across growth, risk, liquidity, tax efficiency, and protection, giving you the clarity to align your portfolio with your vision and risk tolerance.

The lesson of this chapter is clear: financial independence is won by how much you keep, multiply, and safeguard over time. When you master the discipline of compounding, the foresight of diversification, and the wisdom of protection, you build wealth that is not only resilient but enduring. But the quiet power of financial independence: every dollar you have built becomes both a worker and a guard, advancing your future and defending your freedom. As you anchor your journey in this framework, you are accelerating your timeline to FIRE, and also designing a legacy of resilience, strength, and independence that will outlive you.

Wealth and Wisdom Declaration

"Wealth and riches are in their house, and their righteousness endures forever."— Psalm 112:3

Your story carries resilience, and your sacrifices are seeds of abundance.

I boldly declare:

This is my season of strategic growth and divine preservation.

My wealth multiplies daily through compounding wisdom, consistent action, and divine favor.

I walk in financial mastery; building, protecting, and expanding wealth with purpose and precision.

I decree that my money works harder than I do.

I design systems that grow while I rest, multiply while I serve, and sustain me through every season.

I build with foresight and maintain with faithfulness.

I declare that my assets are protected, my risks are managed, and my future is secure.

No storm can destroy what wisdom has built.

No market can shake what grace has fortified.

I confess that every dollar I keep and grow accelerates my financial independence.

I do not consume my harvest before it matures.

I plant, I nurture, I reinvest, and I multiply.

I declare that I create structures that channel income into freedom, not frustration.

My wealth flows through organized systems, strategic portfolios, and Spirit-led stewardship.

Every stream is fortified; every flow is fruitful.

I decree that my tax strategies are efficient, legal, and aligned with long-term vision.

I walk in financial intelligence; honoring both divine and earthly laws.

The wisdom of God governs my counsel, my contracts, and my cashflow.

I affirm that I am disciplined in growth, diligent in protection, and wise in stewardship.

I am not ruled by greed but guided by God's grace.

I guard my wealth without fear and grow it without striving.

I declare that my wealth serves a purpose to fund my dreams, empower others, and impact generations.

My increase is my instrument for influence.

My prosperity has purpose, and my abundance advances the Kingdom.

I confess that I give with intention, aligning my money with my mission and values.

My generosity is strategic.

My giving is guided by revelation.

Every seed I release returns multiplied, protected, and perfected.

I decree that my financial fortress grows stronger every day; shielding my legacy, securing my lineage, and empowering my freedom.

No loss can outpace my restoration.

No attack can breach my divine protection.

I am FIRE'D UP to grow wealth with wisdom, protect it with purpose, and multiply it with mastery.

I live in the overflow of grace, the guidance of God, and the guarantee of legacy.

My wealth is not fleeting; it is fortified.

My riches are not random; they are rooted.

My legacy is not limited; it is lasting. Amen.

Chapter
Seven

THE BEDAZZLED LIFE BY DESIGN
(MONEY WITH MEANING)

B y now, you have learned that financial independence is about alignment, when your money, values, and daily choices move in the same direction. This chapter brings everything together through The Bedazzled Life by Design™ Framework—a practical approach that helps you turn vision into structure and money into a tool for purpose. You will learn how to calculate the cost of your dream life, build income vehicles that sustain it, and keep momentum through habits and systems that feel natural to you.

Freedom, at its core, feels steady. Knowing your plans are working in the background and feeling peace in the rhythm of your life. The Bedazzled Life by Design™ shows you how to create that kind of peace, one that grows from clarity, not circumstance.

Wealth Design

Wealth design is the practice of bringing intention to your financial life. This is how you align money with your vision so that the way you earn, spend, and invest reflects the person you want to become. It brings together who you are, what you value, and how you want to live, and turns those things into daily choices that move you forward.

Instead of collecting scattered tips or random tactics, wealth design builds harmony across every part of your financial world. It helps you see how each decision connects to something larger. You have already started exploring some of these ideas back in Chapter Three. Now, as you move from reflection to design, consider these questions to help you turn meaning into structure:

- What does a great day look like, hour by hour?

- Which values deserve space in my calendar and my spending?

- What outcomes will show I'm on track this quarter and this year?

- Where does my time feel most aligned with who I want to become?

- Which habits or expenses quietly drain the life I'm trying to build?

- What kind of work gives me energy instead of only providing income?

- When I imagine financial freedom, what does it feel like—not just look like?

- Who benefits from the wealth I'm creating, and how do I want that impact to grow?

- How will I know I'm at peace with my pace, my purpose, and my provision?

These questions mark the beginning of your design journey. They help you move from knowing what matters to building a life that reflects it.

The next step is structure, which is a framework that turns ideas into action and intentions into results. That is where The Bedazzled Life by Design™ Framework comes in.

The Bedazzled Life by Design™ Framework

Financial independence is often imagined as a finish line, but few people stop to imagine what freedom looks like in motion. The Bedazzled Life by Design™ Framework was created to close that gap. It turns ideas into a way of living, one that feels purposeful, peaceful, and sustainable.

The name Bedazzled came years earlier, during a conversation with my coach and friend, Debola Deji-Kurunmi (DDK), founder of The Visionary Compass Accelerator Program. She asked me to imagine a life that radiated joy, freedom, and purpose, a life so alive it shimmered. That simple exercise planted a seed. Over time, it grew into the framework you are reading now.

The framework unfolds in four connected parts that build on each other:

● **Discover**: uncover who you are beyond your paycheck.

● **Design**: translate your vision and values into numbers that reflect the life you want.

● **Deploy**: activate the income streams and systems that bring those numbers to life.

● **Drive**: maintain your progress through steady rhythms, personal rules, and consistent review.

This is a working model, something you can practice, adapt, and grow into. People from different backgrounds have used this approach to create lives in which money supports what matters rather than competing with it. You've already done much of the work of discovery in earlier chapters. Now it is time to design, to bring your values and vision into focus through practical, measurable choices.

Design: Translating Vision into Numbers

When I began this process, I found inspiration in Rachel Rodgers' book We Should All Be Millionaires. She challenged readers to stop wishing vaguely and start calculating the real cost of their dream life. That challenge stayed with me. It's one thing to say, "I want to earn $10,000 a month" or "I'll need $3 million to retire," but until you know what those numbers include, they are just guesses. I had to ask: What does my life cost to live well?

How much for my home?

My family's travel.

My wellness?

My creative space?

As I broke it down, I began to see the pieces of my dream life reflected in practical terms, things I could measure, adjust, and plan for. That reflection became the foundation for what I now call The Bedazzled Life by Design™ Framework, a structure built around twelve domains that capture the fullness of a meaningful life.

Each domain represents a part of your daily experience that carries both emotional and financial weight: home, family, health, creativity, giving, and more. Every one of them comes with a cost not just in dollars, but in time and energy. When you put real numbers beside your values, something shifts. Dreams stop floating in abstraction. They become goals with price tags, timelines, and strategy.

Rachel's idea of a "wildcard" category, space for whatever makes your life uniquely yours became one of my favorite parts of the framework. It reminds us that no two visions are identical, and no wealth plan should be either.

How to Calculate Your Freedom Number

Let me show you how this works through Maya's story, a mid-career professional I once coached. At 42, she was a project manager, wife, and mother of two. Her salary was solid, but she often said she felt like she was "getting by" instead of truly living. She had never stopped to ask what it would cost to live her dream life.

When we began mapping her world across The Bedazzled Life by Design™ Framework, we walked through the fourteen domains that make up a meaningful, well-rounded life. These are the same domains you'll reference as you design your own vision, the categories that bring clarity, structure, and balance to your financial picture.

Here's what Maya's dream life looked like when we broke it down together:

- **Home**: a comfortable four-bedroom rental with space for her children to grow, $3,000/month

- **Family**: reliable after-school care and summer programs, $1, 200/month

- **Career/Work:** professional development budget for certifications and conferences, $300/month

- **Food, Health & Wellness:** healthier groceries, organic produce, and weekly meal prep help, $500/month

155

- **Fitness & Movement:** a gym membership and yoga classes, $120/month

- **Education/Personal Development:** courses, coaching, and books, $200/month

- **Office & Workspace:** better lighting, equipment, live plants, wall art, and calming scents, $150/month

- **Clothing & Style:** modest wardrobe updates each season, $100/month.

- **Financial Stability:** insurance, emergency fund contributions, and debt paydown, $800/month

- **Transportation:** car payment, gas, and maintenance, $600/month

- **Travel:** two family trips a year, averaged over twelve months, $700/month

- **Spirituality, Legacy & Impact:** giving to her church and a local nonprofit, $300/month.

- **Entertainment & Joy:** outings, streaming services, and birthdays, $200/month

- **Wildcard:** hobbies or spontaneous adventures, $200/month

When we added it all up, Maya 's dream lifestyle came to about $8,270 per month, or just under $100,000 a year.

Her realization was simple but powerful. She did not need millions to feel free. She didn't need yachts or luxury homes.

She needed clarity. Seeing her life expressed through real numbers gave her the peace she had not felt in years. For the first time, she could see the number that represented her dream: her Freedom Number.

To find it, we multiplied her annual lifestyle cost ($100,000) by 25, giving her a goal of $2.5 million in invested assets. The calculation is based on the 4% rule, which suggests that withdrawing 4% per year from a diversified portfolio can sustain income for decades. Please not that this is not a perfect formula for everyone, but a strong starting point, the one that turns financial independence from an abstract idea into a tangible plan.

Maya's biggest takeaway was what it revealed. Financial peace comes from defining enough. That clarity turned abstract freedom into something she could see, plan for, and build toward every day.

As you move forward, these same twelve to fourteen domains will become the foundation of your own design process. Each one invites you to attach real numbers to what matters most, so your wealth plan reflects not just what you earn, but how you want to live.

The Power of Design

Design brings direction. It helps you see money as more than digits on a screen; it becomes a mirror of your values and a tool for building the life you envision. Once you know the cost of your dream life, decisions start to feel lighter. You no longer wonder what "enough" looks like. You can build around real numbers instead of chasing vague goals.

That's the beauty of this stage. Design helps you take what you've discovered about yourself and translate it into a plan that supports your vision. You begin to design a financial life that feels like it belongs to you steady, intentional, and alive with meaning.

Deploy: Turning Dreams into Income

Design gives you the numbers. 'Deploy' brings them to life. This is where your dream stops being a spreadsheet and starts becoming cash flow.

When I first mapped my Bedazzled Life, I saw the gap between what my salary provided and what my vision required. That's when I realized a paycheck alone could never fund the life I was designing. Salaries offer stability, but they are limited. Dreams demand expansion.

Deploy is the phase where expansion begins. It is about moving your Skills-to-Cash ideas from concept into practice. By now, you have already explored this in Chapter 4, where you identified skills, services, and talents that can become income streams. Deploy does not repeat those lessons. Instead, it calls you to action: choose one or two and set them in motion.

Skills-to-Cash represents the channels through which money flows. A salary is one channel, but your Bedazzled

Life requires more. Research shows that most wealthy individuals sustain three to seven streams of income. The more channels you activate, the stronger and faster your journey toward freedom becomes.

What you need is to carve out fifteen to twenty hours each week in the evenings, on weekends, or even during a lunch break, and dedicate them to building income engines. Week after week, those hours compound into transformation.

My friend Kiki, a mid-career accountant craving flexibility. Her schedule revolved around client deadlines, quarterly reports, and late-night reconciliations. She loved her work but hated how it consumed her evenings with her kids. When we mapped her Bedazzled Life, she realized what she really wanted was margin, time to be present without guilt. So, she began tutoring high school students online in math and accounting concepts for just ten hours a week. It wasn't glamorous, but it was hers. Within six months, her tutoring brought in $1,200 a month, enough to fund her family's travel expenses. For the first time, she booked a summer trip without touching her main paycheck. That single change gave her a taste of freedom that no salary increases ever had.

Then there is Daniel, a corporate marketer who felt stuck in repetition. His nine-to-five was stable but uninspiring. Outside work, he loved creating sleek presentation templates for friends and small businesses. When he realized those designs could become digital products, he packaged them into a set of professional templates and listed them online. It took a few weekends to polish and upload, but within months, sales started rolling in. His product now earns about $500 a month in passive income enough to cover his fitness, wellness, and personal development domains. More importantly, it reminded him that his creativity had value beyond his job title. That realization reignited his drive in both business and life.

Start small, test, iterate, and refine. The professionals who thrive here are not always the most brilliant; they are the most consistent. They treat their side ventures like a laboratory, running experiments, learning from the results, and multiplying their vehicles over time. The goal is to close the gap between your current reality and your Bedazzled Life.

Each dollar earned outside your paycheck is a dollar that funds freedom, family, wellness, travel, legacy and purpose. Deploy requires courage, but it also requires structure. Protect your time. Commit to one or two Skills-to-Cash projects this quarter. Test them. Refine them. Repeat. Because dreams do not fund themselves. Deploy is the bridge between vision and reality, the place where your Bedazzled Life begins to pay for itself.

Drive: Consistency Beats Intensity

Discovery helped you see who you are. Design gave you structure. Deploy sets your vision in motion. Drive is what sustains it. This stage is where freedom moves from sheer excitement to rhythm. Lasting change rarely comes from big leaps; it comes from steady habits that compound over time.

Bedazzled Life unfolds through consistent routines that builds confidence piece by piece. My Weekly Wealthness Check; a 60-to-90-minute session to review goals and finances became the anchor that kept me aligned. So did Strategic Sundays and Quarterly Reviews. Small rituals, repeated with intention, have a quiet power.

Drive is about pacing yourself with steady movement, not sprints. This is the rhythm that keeps your wealth journey alive long after the excitement fades.

The 30/60/90 Execution Grid

Drive thrives on cycles. Treat every quarter as a 90-day runway for progress—test, learn, refine.

- **30 Days:** Start one income experiment, trim one expense that doesn't serve your vision, and automate one financial task.

- **60 Days:** Add fuel to what's working. Increase contributions, reinvest profits, or bring in accountability partners.

- **90 Days:** Reflect and realign. In the FIRE'D UU framework, this means you:

- Refine what's working and sharpen it.

161

- Reignite what has potential but needs more attention.

- Release what no longer serves your goals.

This rhythm keeps your design alive. You're not waiting for a distant milestone; you're practicing freedom now, one quarter at a time.

Personal Operating Rules

Drive also requires guardrails, simple boundaries that protect your vision when life gets busy. These rules help your values stay in charge of your calendar.

A few examples:

- Invest before upgrading your lifestyle.

- Give before you spend.

- Block off evenings for rest or family time.

- Keep two afternoons each week meeting-free.

They don't have to be complicated. The power is in honoring them. When your daily decisions match your long-term values, you create stability that lasts.

Your Weekly Wealthness Check ensures your habits remain consistent. Over time, consistency reshapes who you are and how you handle money.

Drive is the stage where freedom becomes part of your identity. You begin to live with alignment rather than striving toward it. Consistency anchors your progress, turning effort into peace and daily choices into legacy.

Money With Meaning, Stewardship and Purpose

At the heart of The Bedazzled Life by Design™ lies a truth I hold close: true wealth is alignment. Alignment with vision. Alignment with values, and for those who are believers, alignment with God's purpose for our lives.

Everything we have begins with Him. Scripture reminds us, "Remember the Lord your God, for it is He who gives you the ability to produce wealth" (Deuteronomy 8:18). That truth reframes ownership. We are not owners but stewards, caretakers of resources meant to serve His plans.

We are called not only to pay bills or pursue comfort but to fund God's assignments, sustain generosity, and support the visions He is entrusted to us. When you understand wealth as stewardship, every financial decision becomes spiritual. Earning becomes an act of obedience. Giving becomes an act of worship. Saving and investing become acts of trust. Each one says, *"I believe what I've been given has purpose."*

In finance, we often talk about return on investment. In a life of alignment, the measure runs deeper: return on integrity. When your spending, giving, and investing reflect what you believe, every decision carries meaning.

When your purchases reflect your priorities, even small things bring contentment. When your giving matches your heart, every contribution feels like a seed planted in faith. Money was never meant to define us. It becomes what it was always meant to be a tool. Not a master, not an identity, not the measure of worth, but an instrument to build, bless, and create impact.

God's provision was never meant to stop at your household. It was meant to flow through you to fund ideas, support others, and advance good in the world. The highest expression of wealth contribution. This is what it means to live a Bedazzled Life by Design: a life where money serves mission, and stewardship becomes worship.

Action Steps: Designing Your Bedazzled Life

We have learned that knowledge is valuable, but action creates change.

Here are five steps to help you put the Bedazzled Life by Design™ framework into practice.

1. *Write Your Bedazzled Life Vision*

In five to seven sentences, describe the life you'd be proud to live on repeat. Picture your mornings and evenings. Imagine how you spend your workdays, your weekends, your quiet moments.

Write how it feels not just what it looks like. Let clarity matter more than perfection. This becomes your compass for every financial and life decision that follows.

2. *Put a Price Tag on Your Dream*

Break your vision into the fourteen domains we listed earlier: home, family, health, travel, giving, and more. Estimate the monthly cost for each, then add them together to find your Dream Lifestyle Cost.

Multiply that number by twelve for your annual figure, then by twenty-five to find your Freedom Number. This simple calculation turns "someday" into something measurable.

3. *Start One Income Engine*

Choose one or two income streams you can begin this quarter. Protect ten to fifteen hours each week in the evenings, on weekends, or during early mornings to build and test your new source of income. Don't wait for the perfect plan. Start small, stay consistent, and let momentum grow.

Progress matters more than scale. If you need ideas, revisit the Skills-to-Cash section in Chapter 4 for examples of services, creative work, and other ways to turn your skills into cash flow.

4. *Establish Your Weekly Wealthness Check*

Set aside sixty to ninety minutes each week to look your money in the eye. Review your accounts, track your progress, and reconnect your numbers to your vision. This habit turns anxiety into clarity. Treat this time as sacred it's where confidence compounds.

5. *Anchor Your Values with Rules*

Write three to five personal rules that protect your vision when life gets noisy.

Examples:

● Invest before upgrading your lifestyle.

● Give before spending.

● No work emails after 8 p.m.

● These rules become quiet guardrails simple, but powerful enough to keep your life aligned with what matters most.

Start here. Just these five steps will set your design in motion. Small, steady choices compound faster than grand plans. With each week of alignment, your Bedazzled Life begins to move off the page and into reality.

Chapter Summary

Your Bedazzled Life by Design™ isn't something to chase in the future; it's something you can start living now. This chapter showed how to move from paycheck-driven choices to a life guided by vision, values, and freedom.

It begins with Discover, where you reclaim your identity beyond job titles and responsibilities. Discovery invites you to pause, listen, and clarify what truly matters. Once that happens, money finds its rightful place as a resource that serves your purpose rather than defining it.

Next comes Design, the phase that turns reflection into structure. Through the fourteen domains, you learn to measure what a meaningful life costs and calculate your Freedom Number. Independence stops being an idea and becomes a plan you can act on.

Deploy is where that plan begins to move. You put your skills, creativity, and resources to work to create income streams that match your goals. This stage is about courage, consistency, and forward motion, turning potential into progress.

Drive keeps everything steady. Freedom isn't built in a sprint; it's shaped through rhythm and repetition. Practices like the 30/60/90 Execution Grid, Weekly Wealthness Checks, and clear personal rules keep your growth grounded in discipline and peace.

Finally, Money with Meaning brings it all home. Stewardship, generosity, and alignment remind us that money has a spiritual purpose. It was never meant to control or consume; it was meant to build, bless, and create impact. Every decision earning, saving, giving, or investing becomes an act of integrity.

Together, these phases form a rhythm for living well. The Bedazzled Life by Design™ is all about significance. When your money reflects your faith, values, and vision, wealth stops being a goal and becomes a byproduct of a life well lived.

Wealth and Wisdom Declaration

Habakkuk 2:2 — "Write the vision and make it plain on tablets, that he may run who reads it."

Proverbs 24:3–4 — "By wisdom a house is built, and through understanding it is established; through knowledge its rooms are filled with rare and beautiful treasures."

Your life will either happen by default or by design. These declarations remind you that you have the power to shape your lifestyle, your finances, and your future. Speak them boldly to anchor yourself in the truth that wealth is not the end goal but the architect's tool to build the life you were called to live.

I boldly declare:

My life will not happen by default; it unfolds by divine design.

I am the architect of a purposeful, prosperous, and peaceful life.

With clarity of vision and discipline of spirit, I design the life I desire and deserve.

I decree that my life is designed with clarity, purpose, and intention—never left to chance.

I refuse to drift through destiny. Every day I build deliberately, guided by divine direction.

I declare that my money aligns with my vision.

Finances serve me—they do not master me.

I am no longer enslaved by hustle or fear. I am led by purpose, peace, and precision.

I affirm that every decision I make today shapes the abundant life I will live tomorrow.

My habits are holy blueprints. My plans are prophetic patterns.

I move with foresight and act with faith.

I confess that I reject a life of default.

I embrace a designed life—crafted with meaning, joy, and freedom.

I refuse mediocrity; I choose mastery. I refuse chaos; I choose clarity.

I decree that I design systems that sustain both my wealth and my well-being.

My lifestyle is not a reaction; it is a reflection of intentional vision.

My routines are rooted in wisdom, and my outcomes are anchored in order.

I declare that my vision is sharper than my fears.

I am not moved by pressure; I am led by purpose.

I make decisions with confidence, courage, and conviction.

I affirm that my wealth fuels my purpose, my family's flourishing, and my legacy for generations.

Money is not my motive—it is my ministry's multiplier.

Through me, divine resources meet divine assignments.

I confess that clarity comes before tactics.

When vision leads, provision follows.

As I refine my focus, my plan simplifies, and my path strengthens.

I decree that I live a balanced life—faith first, family next, health guarded, and freedom preserved.

These are my pillars of prosperity and peace.

I am not just wealthy; I am whole.

I declare that my life is a masterpiece of divine design—funded by abundance, framed by purpose, and finished in fulfillment.

I walk in beauty, wisdom, and grace.

I live a life that glows with meaning and grows with momentum.

My story is one of alignment, my wealth is one of legacy, and my life is one of light.

I am FIRE'D UP to live designed life not by default, but by destiny.

I am building the Bedazzled Life, crafted by purpose, sustained by wisdom, and crowned with glory. Amen.

PART III

—

THE ACCELERATION PLAN
(ROADMAP & TOOLS)

Chapter
Eight

NOTES TO IMMIGRANTS BUILDING TRANSGENERATIONAL WEALTH

The Courage to Begin Again

You may remember the two suitcases I carried into America. The checked bag got lighter as life settled. The other one the one packed with legacy and sacrifice gained weight. I began to understand that I was building more than my own life. I was laying down a path for my children, my community, and every immigrant who dares to believe financial independence is possible.

Behind me was everything familiar: the rhythm of my homeland, the comfort of my language, and the steady presence of family. Ahead of me stood uncertainty. Would my accent hold me back in professional rooms? Would my degrees still matter here? Could I stand on my own without the safety net I once knew?

My story is not entirely unique. According to the Migration Policy Institute (2023), nearly 45 million immigrants live in the United States, about 14 percent of the population. Some arrive with advanced degrees and begin in low-wage jobs. Others arrive with little formal education and build thriving businesses through grit. Sacrifice shapes nearly every immigrant story, not as tragedy, but as the starting point for rebuilding.

For many of us, failure feels generational. We are not only chasing our own dreams. We carry the hopes of parents who gave up comfort, the prayers of children we promised a better future, and the expectations of families watching from afar. That weight can break a person or shape a person. For me, it shaped me.

Starting at the Bottom, Dreaming at the Top

You may remember from earlier in this book how my journey began: studying while nursing a newborn, balancing two toddlers and two degrees, and finding strength in exhaustion. Those years were my first classroom in resilience. They taught lessons no syllabus could cover, like how to manage time when there was never enough of it, how to stretch one income across too many needs, and how to keep moving even when doubt whispered louder than hope.

I came to America as a graduate student, a wife, and a

mother of two little ones. My husband was still back home, so I lived in a small apartment, carrying both the dream and the daily grind. Some days, I studied with one child napping on my lap and another tugging at my sleeve. Some nights, I balanced textbooks on the edge of my bed while nursing my newborn. The nights were long, and the mornings even longer.

Exhaustion often left me in tears, but quitting was never an option.

There were moments when I questioned everything. The weight of responsibility pressed hard, but purpose always won. Would this degree open doors? Was leaving my homeland worth it? Could I be a student, a mother, and the family breadwinner at once?

When I finally walked across the stage at graduation, it was more than a ceremony. It was evidence that barriers bend under persistence. Immigrants are not defined by limitation; we are shaped by resilience.

Looking back, I realize those years trained me for financial independence. Juggling classes, childcare, and cultural adjustment became a masterclass in endurance and focus. Those skills, including time management, discipline, and adaptability, became the foundation for building wealth and stability later.

Immigrants often start at the bottom regardless of qualifications. Degrees earned abroad are questioned.

Accents are scrutinized. Experience is undervalued. According to the Migration Policy Institute, nearly two million highly educated immigrants in the United States are unemployed or working in low-skill jobs because their credentials are not recognized. Many of us swallow our pride and start again.

A first job does not define destiny. It can serve as a launching pad. The American dream rarely looks glamorous at the beginning. It looks like night shifts, second jobs, and studying after work when your body begs for sleep. Those sacrifices act like investments. They compound. The resilience forged in those seasons becomes the foundation of financial independence.

Immigrant Advantages: Turning Identity into Strategy

When I left my homeland to start over in the United States, I discovered that immigrant identity is a toolkit. Inside it, I found resilience shaped by storms I had already weathered, adaptability from navigating unfamiliar worlds, and a global perspective that widened every room I entered. These were accelerants for wealth building.

Corporations pay consultants to teach problem-solving under pressure, cross-cultural communication, and persistence in the face of uncertainty. Immigrants practice these skills daily. We know how to make something out of nothing. We know how to pivot. We know how to push through discomfort because we have already uprooted our lives once before.

Research echoes this reality. The National Bureau of Economic Research reports that immigrant-founded businesses in the United States generate more than $1.6 trillion in annual revenue and employ over 8 million people. Immigrants are not only participating in economies. We are accelerating them.

Resilience as Wealth Strategy

Every immigrant understands resilience. We live it. We hear it in our accents, feel it when learning new languages as adults, and prove it when starting over in careers where credentials go unrecognized. We show it when raising children without the family support structures, we once relied on. Resilience is more than survival. It functions as a transferable wealth strategy.

The tears, rejections, and long nights balancing a baby in one arm and textbooks in the other now look different to me. They trained creativity, discipline, and endurance. Financial independence requires all three.

Across the globe, immigrant resilience has produced extraordinary wealth creation.

- Indra Nooyi left India carrying more than ambition; she carried the pressure of representing every woman who would come after her. She rose through the ranks of corporate America until she became CEO of

PepsiCo, leading a global company while balancing motherhood, identity, and an accent in rooms where few looked or sounded like her. Her story is a reminder that leadership is not just about position but about presence — about showing that excellence can speak in any accent.

- Hamdi Ulukaya arrived from Turkey and saw potential where others saw failure. He bought a shuttered yogurt factory in upstate New York with borrowed money and built it into Chobani, a brand known as much for its heart as its success. He hired refugees, offered them equity, and created an ecosystem where business and compassion could coexist. His journey proved that reinvention is not luck; it is the discipline to see value where others see waste.

- Sergey Brin came to the United States as a child refugee from the Soviet Union, carrying both curiosity and displacement. Years later, he co-founded Google, a company that reshaped how the world searches for knowledge. His path reflects a truth many immigrants know: when you grow up between worlds, you learn to question how things work and imagine how they could work better.

These stories are proof of what happens when resilience meets opportunity. Everyday examples carry the same power, even if they attract fewer headlines. The determination to keep applying after rejection until one "yes" arrives. The discipline to navigate a foreign credit system to buy a first home. The courage to build a side hustle on top of a full-time job because one paycheck feels too fragile.

Financial independence rarely goes to those who never fall. It grows with each rise after a fall. Immigrants know how to rise. We adapt quickly and try again. Resilience builds the bridge between hardship and breakthrough.

Why Immigrants Are Wired for FIRE

Immigrants already understand how to adapt, innovate, and bridge worlds. The same qualities that help us survive new cultures also shape how we save, invest, and build. Adaptability sharpens decision-making when careers or markets shift. A global perspective opens opportunities across borders, from real estate to entrepreneurship. As diversity advocate Verna Myers said, "Diversity is being invited to the party; inclusion is being asked to dance."

For immigrants, inclusion means more than belonging. It means building wealth that keeps our seat at the table for generations to come. When we start viewing our cultural differences as assets instead of obstacles, those traits become a strategy. Our accents, perspectives, and lived experiences are not limitations. They are the leverage, unique advantages that make financial independence both attainable and practical.

If FIRE, Financial Independence, Retire Early, were a

language, immigrants would already speak it fluently. Everything the FIRE movement teaches sacrificing today for freedom tomorrow, creating multiple streams of income, and investing with long-term vision has been part of our story all along. We did not learn these lessons from books. We learned them in transition and in sacrifice. We learned from the courage it took to start over.

The Data Speaks

Numbers tell the same story our lives already prove. According to the Kauffman Foundation, immigrants make up nearly one in four new entrepreneurs in the United States, even though we represent only about fourteen percent of the population. We are almost twice as likely to start businesses as those born here. For many, entrepreneurship is not a luxury. It is survival turned into strategy.

Globally, the pattern repeats itself. Immigrants fuel economic growth not only by contributing labor but by creating new enterprises, building innovations, and sustaining cross-border economies through remittances. The World Bank reports that in 2023, remittances to low-and middle-income countries exceeded $669 billion 2023, stabilizing entire economies. Those funds paid for education, housing, and small businesses, keeping entire families and communities afloat.

Behind every statistic is a familiar rhythm: discipline, sacrifice, and long-term vision. These traits are the same foundation that the FIRE movement celebrates. Immigrants have been practicing them for generations, often without naming them as financial principles. What others describe as financial independence, we recognize as the mindset that helped us survive and eventually thrive.

The Immigrant Mindset

Immigrants stretch one dollar into five. We build bridges across cultures. We create opportunities where none seem to exist. The habits that once helped us survive are the same ones that help us build wealth. Across the world, the story looks familiar.

- Many African immigrants use rotating savings systems to fund businesses or buy property.

- Many Filipino immigrants pool family resources to acquire real estate both in the United States and back home.

- Many Chinese immigrant families run businesses where everyone contributes, building stability together.

These traditions predate the FIRE movement. They reflect the same principles of community, discipline, and long-term vision that define financial independence.

Immigrants think in decades, not days. We left comfort to build something lasting. We know how to take risks, adapt when plans shift, and start again when we must. For me, FIRE simply gave language to what I was already practicing.

Depending on one paycheck felt fragile. Creating multiple streams of income felt necessary. FIRE helped turn those instincts into a system—a way to transform sacrifice into strategy and endurance into sustainable wealth.

Immigrants are well-positioned for financial independence because we already know what it means to rebuild. Reinvention is part of our story. Every time we rise after rejection or find opportunity in scarcity, we strengthen the foundation for the generations that follow. FIRE fits naturally into that rhythm it gives structure to what many of us have lived all along.

And among those who carry that story, immigrant women often bear it twice over balancing ambition and expectation, responsibility, and reinvention.

A Word to Immigrant Women

For immigrant women, the climb is steeper. We carry more than the weight of ambition. We balance cultures, families, and expectations, often in systems that do not see the full scope of our strength. We navigate gender bias and cultural pressure while trying to build lives that honor both where we came from and where we are going.

I remember walking into classrooms with my baby strapped to my back because childcare had fallen through. I felt the stares and the quiet judgment, wondering if I belonged there. Now, I see those moments differently. They were lessons in endurance. My children learned from watching me push through exhaustion. Determination is not something we teach but what we live.

The data reflects what many of us already know. Immigrant women often earn less than native-born women but are more likely to be self-employed. When the traditional doors do not open, we build our own. That persistence is not accidental. It is instinct. We have learned how to stretch what we have, plan for tomorrow, and create new paths when none exist.

For us, financial independence is more than a milestone. It is a promise to the next generation. Every dollar saved, every investment made, every stream of income created carries meaning. It says, *"I will not pass down survival alone. I will pass down choice."*

FIRE is not just a financial goal for immigrant women it is an act of restoration. It repairs what scarcity once broke. It gives our children a new story to inherit. Each time one woman rises, she pulls another with her. Our strength multiplies through community, and our victories ripple forward.

Immigrant women are not only part of the wealth conversation. We are shaping it. Our resilience is generational. Our progress does not end with us. It becomes the foundation our daughters and sons will stand on.

Visa and Residency as Financial Strategy: What to Know and How to Plan

The immigrant journey is rarely a straight road. It is filled with detours, delays, and demands that many of our peers will never fully understand. Visas decide where we can work, how long we can stay, and whether we can build something of our own. Employers may question our accents or underestimate our competence. Many of us accept jobs far below our qualifications just to get a foothold, all while sending money home to prove that the dream we pursued was real.

This weight is unique because it is not carried for us alone. It is generational. We hold the expectations of parents who set aside their own ambitions, the dependence of relatives who rely on our remittances, and the watchful eyes of children who look to us for stability. According to the World Bank (2023), immigrants sent home more than $669 billion in remittances globally. For some households in developing countries, these transfers account for over 20 percent of total income.

Acts of love like these strengthen families and communities abroad, yet they often come with a hidden cost: every dollar sent home is one less invested in building wealth where we live.

I remember moments of deep discouragement when my credentials were dismissed and rejection letters arrived one after another, each beginning with "unfortunately."

Sitting in interviews, I sometimes felt invisible, as if my worth had been lost in translation. Those moments could have broken me, but they shaped me instead. They taught me to reframe my identity. My accent became proof of courage. My background became my advantage. My setbacks became lessons in resourcefulness. What I once tried to hide became the very thing that set me apart.

Visas as Financial Roadmaps

Immigration paperwork defines where you can work, how long you can stay, and the kind of wealth you can build. The type of visa you hold shapes opportunities and limitations at the same time. Many immigrants wait for stability before making financial moves, yet stability often grows through the process of building, not before it.

According to Pew Research (2023), more than one million immigrants in the United States live and work on temporary visas such as H-1B, L-1, and O-1. Each visa opens doors in different ways while setting its own boundaries.

- **H-1B Visa:** Allows highly skilled professionals to work in the U.S. but limits entrepreneurship. It supports employment, not business ownership.

- **L-1 Visa:** Designed for intra-company transfers. Spouses on L-2 visas may apply for work authorization, which can lead to family-run ventures.

- **O-1 Visa:** For individuals with exceptional ability

in science, art, education, or business. It provides flexibility for those with specialized expertise.

Ada came from Lagos to Silicon Valley on an H-1B visa as an engineer. While waiting for her green card, she learned she could not start her own company under her visa.

Instead of putting her goals aside, she worked within her reality. She used her spouse's L-2 visa, which allowed work authorization, to launch a small consulting practice. Over the next three years, she expanded it, transitioned into venture investing, and eventually managed a $50 million fund. Ada did not let her visa define her path. She built progress within its boundaries and created new possibilities for herself and her family.

Overlooked Pathways

Many immigrants are unaware of additional routes that can accelerate their financial position. Each of these programs offers opportunities for stability and long-term planning when approached with strategy and foresight.

- **EB-5 Visa:** A direct route to permanent residency through investment. By investing between $800,000 and $1,050,000 in U.S. businesses that create jobs, immigrants can secure a green card for themselves and their families.

- **International Entrepreneur Parole (IEP):** Grants a temporary stay for entrepreneurs whose startups show strong potential to create jobs and benefit the U.S. economy.

- **E-2 Treaty Investor Visa:** Available to nationals of certain countries, it allows individuals to develop and manage businesses in which they have invested.

- **Diversity Visa Lottery (Green Card Lottery):** A chance-based program that, while limited, opens the door to permanent residency for thousands each year.

These pathways reveal a larger truth: a visa is not only documentation. It can also serve as a financial framework. When understood and used strategically, it becomes a key part of your wealth-building roadmap.

Aligning Visa Timelines with Wealth Timelines

Think of your visa as more than an immigration status. It can also serve as a financial planning tool. Track visa deadlines with the same care you give to bill payments or investment dates. Align your residency timeline with your financial independence goals so that both move in the same direction.

If your visa limits your ability to pursue entrepreneurship, use that season to build credibility in your field, save intentionally, and invest in education or certifications that will strengthen your next step. If your spouse's visa allows more flexibility, explore business opportunities that you can pursue together. If permanent residency is on the horizon, treat that waiting period as preparation time for long-term investments, real estate, or ventures that will grow over decades.

The earlier you plan, the more time you give your wealth to compound. Understanding your visa gives you an edge that many overlook. What begins as a set of restrictions can become a platform for freedom when approached with creativity, discipline, and foresight.

Review the list below to see how you can align your visa and wealth timeline:

Visa Type   Opportunities Financial Limitations
FIRE Strategy Alignment

VISA TYPE	OPPORTUNITIES	FINANCIAL LIMITATIONS	FIRE STRATEGY ALIGNMENT
H-1B (Skilled Worker)	Employment in specialized fields; pathway to green card through employer sponsorship	Entrepreneurship restricted; income tied to employer	Maximize savings, invest early, and pursue employer sponsored green card for long-term freedom
L-1 (Intra-Company Transfer)	Transfer within multinational companies; spouse (L-2) may gain work authorization	Holder restricted to employer; entrepreneurship depends on spouse's status	Leverage spouse's L-2 authorization for entrepreneurship; build wealth through dual-income strategy
O-1 (Extraordinary Ability)	Work authorization for individuals with exceptional ability in sciences, arts, or business	Work authorization for individuals with exceptional ability in sciences, arts, or business	Capitalize on high-income potential during visa validity; plan for stability via green card
EB-5 (Investor Visa)	Direct route to permanent residency through significant investment in U.S. businesses	Temporary, tied to proven ability; renewal required	Fastest path to green card; ideal for high-net-worth immigrants seeking stability and generational wealth
IEP (International Entrepreneur Parole)	Temporary stay for startup founders who can create jobs and growth	Requires $800,000–$1,050,000 investment; high threshold	Use period to validate and scale business ideas; prepare backup plan for long-term residency
E-2 (Treaty Investor Visa)	Allows nationals of treaty countries to develop and direct businesses with substantial investment	Only available to nationals of eligible countries; investment must be "at risk"	Launch and grow businesses aligned with FIRE goals; plan ahead for permanent residency
Diversity Visa Lottery	Random selection grants permanent residency (green card)	Chance-based; no guarantee of selection	If selected, unlocks full access to entrepreneurship, property, and long-term FIRE strategy

Beyond the U.S.: A Global View of Visas and Financial Strategy

While much of this discussion centers on the United States, immigrants around the world face similar realities. Visas and residency rules shape not only where we live, but also how we work, build wealth, and plan.

In every region, North America, Europe, the Middle East, or Asia-Pacific, a visa is more than a travel document but a framework that defines access, ownership, and opportunity.

Each country structures its immigration system differently, but the financial implications are universal:

- **Canada**: Permanent residency through the Express Entry system or Provincial Nominee Programs often requires proof of funds. Many immigrants use this as a built-in savings discipline, creating an early financial cushion before they arrive. Canada also offers the Start-Up Visa Program for entrepreneurs backed by Canadian investors.

- **United Kingdom:** The Skilled Worker Visa provides employment opportunities but limits access to public benefits. The Innovator Founder Visa offers a path for entrepreneurs to build businesses and, with time, transition to Indefinite Leave to Remain, unlocking long-term stability and wealth potential.

- **Australia:** The Skilled Independent Visa (subclass

189) and Employer Nomination Scheme both lead to permanent residency for skilled professionals. The Business Innovation and Investment Visa supports entrepreneurial immigrants who contribute to the local economy.

- **European Union:** Countries such as Portugal and Spain offer Golden Visa Programs that link residency to investment in real estate or business. These programs allow families to build assets while gaining stability and freedom of movement across the region.

- **United Arab Emirates (UAE):** The UAE's 10-Year Golden Visa for investors, entrepreneurs, and highly skilled professionals provides stability in a tax-free environment, encouraging long-term investment in property and business. Short-term work visas remain common, but the Golden Visa is changing how immigrants build financial roots.

- **Singapore:** As one of Asia's leading financial hubs, Singapore offers the Employment Pass for professionals and the EntrePass for entrepreneurs. Both pathways provide residency and connect immigrants to a thriving, globally linked economy.

- **New Zealand:** The Skilled Migrant Category Resident Visa grants permanent residency to qualified professionals. Entrepreneurial and investor visas create additional opportunities for those seeking both lifestyle stability and long-term financial growth.

The global takeaway is simple: your residency status directly shapes your financial path. The earlier you understand what your visa allows and the opportunities it can unlock the more strategically you can plan for independence.

For the immigrant professional in London, Lagos, Toronto, Sydney, Dubai, Singapore, or Auckland, the same principles apply:

- Know the details of your visa.

- Treat it as part of your financial roadmap.

- Align its timeline with your wealth goals.

Optimizing Cross-Border Finances

For many immigrants, sending money home is not a choice. Parents depend on it for food and medical care. Siblings rely on it for tuition. Communities depend on it to build homes, businesses, and places of worship. These transfers are acts of love, yet without strategy, they can quietly drain the wealth we are working so hard to create.

Here are three ways to make remittances more effective:

1. *Audit Your Transfers.*

Review your last six to twelve months of payments. How much did you send, and how much disappeared in fees? Awareness is the first step toward keeping more of what you earn.

2. **Use Low-Cost Platforms.**

Services like Wise, OFX, and Remitly often charge less than one percent, compared to traditional banks' 3 to 5 percent. Over time, that difference becomes real savings.

3. **Balance Giving with Investing.**

Set aside a portion of your income for long-term growth where you live. A healthy investment portfolio allows you to give more sustainably later.

Remittances should not only flow out they should also build something that endures. When managed wisely, they can uplift families abroad and strengthen your foundation at home.

Generosity is part of who we are, but empowerment comes from balance. Giving and building do not compete; they work together. When both move in harmony, our support for loved ones today becomes the seed of independence for tomorrow.

Bicultural Networks for Opportunity: Leveraging Your Two Worlds

One of the most overlooked advantages immigrants have been the strength of dual networks. We live between two worlds deeply connected to the country we came from and rooted in the country we now call home. When used with intention, that identity is not a barrier but a bridge. It opens doors that others may never even notice.

María, an immigrant from Bogotá, understood this early on. While living in the United States, she began purchasing undervalued properties in smaller cities markets many locals ignored. At the same time, she partnered with family members back in Colombia to invest in emerging neighborhoods. By combining her U.S. credit access with her family's local knowledge, she doubled her net worth in five years. María didn't just live in two worlds; she built wealth across them.

Stories like hers are increasingly common. Across the globe, immigrants are using their bicultural advantage in creative and powerful ways:

● Diaspora Chambers of Commerce. Groups like the Nigerian-American Chamber of Commerce and the Hispanic Alliance for Career Enhancement create trade and mentorship pipelines across countries.

● Professional Associations. Immigrant professionals often form networks that link them with global clients, investors, and mentors who understand both markets.

● Joint Ventures. Partnerships with entrepreneurs back home can spark import-export ventures, technology collaborations, or real estate projects that connect two economies.

According to the Brookings Institution, diaspora communities collectively generate tens of billions of dollars each year through cross-border trade and investment often more than formal foreign aid. What might look like small family ventures are driving global economic growth.

Your bicultural identity is a source of leverage. It gives you the ability to move between cultures, to speak multiple languages of business and belonging. It earns you credibility in places where others have no access. It helps you see opportunities others overlook.

The right question is no longer, "Do I fit in?" but "How can I use my two worlds to build something lasting?" When immigrants learn to think this way, our networks stop being a safety net and start becoming engines of opportunity. That is the kind of advantage that builds freedom, accelerates wealth, and strengthens generations to come.

Overcoming Cultural Money Scripts

For many immigrants, the biggest barriers to financial independence are not external. They are internal. They live in the quiet beliefs we inherited from our cultures and families the "money scripts" that shape how we think, save, and spend without us realizing it.

In many of our homes, money was treated with caution or silence. We were taught to save every coin, avoid risk, and never speak openly about finances. These lessons came from love. They protected our parents in unstable economies. But in a new context, they can keep us from growing.

I once met an immigrant professional who told me, "My parents taught me to save every penny but never how to make that penny work." That sentence has stayed with me. Saving matters but saving alone cannot build wealth. To create financial independence, we must learn to make money multiply, not just preserve it.

The Global Financial Literacy Excellence Center found that only one in three adults worldwide is financially literate. Among immigrants, that number is often lower because of language barriers, limited access, or cultural silence around money. Without financial education, fear takes the lead. We avoid investing because it feels uncertain. We stay in jobs that underpay because they feel safe. We hold back on business ideas because failure feels too costly.

Breaking these old patterns takes intention. It begins with courage and continues through consistent conversation. We must retrain how we see and use money not as something to hide or fear, but as a tool we can learn to master.

Here are a few ways to begin rewriting your financial story:

1. **Host Family Financial Summits.**

Meet quarterly with your spouse, children, or extended family to review budgets, set goals, and celebrate wins. Talking about money openly removes the shame and builds unity.

2. *Share Your Story.*

Be honest about what has worked and what hasn't. When you share your experiences, you replace silence with wisdom. Money becomes a shared journey instead of a private struggle.

3. *Teach the Next Generation.*

Go beyond "save your money." Show your children what investing means. Let them see you diversify income, grow assets, and make thoughtful choices. Teach them that money can serve a purpose and create freedom.

This practice changed my own household. When my children were young, I started holding family money talks. They saw me plan for investments, ask questions about opportunities, and set goals for our future. Slowly, the topic of money shifted from tension to trust. They learned that money is not something to hide. It is something to steward. FIRE requires a new script, one rooted in growth, ownership, and courage. A script that replaces fear with faith, silence with strategy, and limitation with possibility. This new money script empowers us not only to build wealth but also to pass down a mindset that outlasts money itself.

The immigrant author Carlos Bulosan once wrote, *"We are all driven by the same dream: to build, to create, to live freely."* To live freely, we must first think freely about money.

The Ripple Effect of Legacy

Legacy holds its greatest power when it becomes a mindset. Assets can be spent, houses can be sold, and businesses can rise and fall. When we pass on the conviction that financial freedom is possible, we give our children something no one can take away. We give them the courage to dream beyond our reach and the wisdom to turn those dreams into reality.

For me, legacy begins at home. My children watch every decision I make about money, work, and faith. They see me choose long-term vision over short-term comfort. They know that I am not only working for income but for freedom. Once modeled, that freedom spreads. They are learning that financial independence is not about wealth for its own sake it is about choices, opportunities, and the dignity to live fully.

Legacy grows through conversation, intention, and example. Every home purchased, every business launched, and every investment made is a declaration that we will pass on wealth, not only struggle. A legacy rooted in financial independence outlives accounts and properties. It builds vision in those who come after us, grounded in purpose, generosity, and stewardship.

Immigrants are reshaping the collective story of wealth and independence for those who will follow. It leaves a framework for the next generation and proves that financial independence is not reserved for the privileged few. It belongs to anyone willing to sacrifice, strategize, and stay the course.

What we build in our adopted countries ripples outward, shaping economies, inspiring others, and lighting a path for those who follow. We are not only surviving. We are designing legacies that endure.

Building Transgenerational Wealth

We work hard, we save, we invest, but without intentional planning, our assets may never serve the next generation. Some families leave behind wealth. Others leave behind confusion, conflict, or debt. The choices you make today will become the legacy your family inherits tomorrow.

Here are four essential tools every immigrant professional should put in place:

- **Wills and Trusts.** Without them, courts and government agencies decide what happens to your assets. With them, you protect your family and ensure your values guide every decision.

- **Retirement Accounts.** 401(k)s, IRAs, and pensions should always have designated beneficiaries. Without this, accounts can be frozen, leaving your loved ones without access when they need it most.

- **Real Estate and Savings.** Secure your property with clear titles, joint ownership, or trusts to make sure it transfers smoothly to those you intend.

- **Life Insurance.** This is one of the most immediate ways to create generational wealth. With proper coverage, you can pass down financial stability overnight.

If you do not create a plan, the system will create one for you—and too often, it erases the very progress your family worked so hard to build.

Action Steps

1. *Audit and Align Your Finances*

Take inventory of all assets, debts, income, and expenses. Clarity is the foundation of progress. Once you know where you stand, align your financial habits with your long-term vision of independence and legacy.

2. *Turn Your Immigrant Identity into Strategy*

Your resilience, adaptability, and global perspective are accelerators. Use these traits to push through barriers, spot opportunities, and build wealth across borders.

3. *Treat Visa and Residency as Part of Your Wealth Plan*

Do not separate your immigration status from your financial strategy. Understand the opportunities and limits of your visa or residency, and plan your career, business, and investments in alignment with it.

4. *Protect and Plan for Legacy*

Secure your family's future through wills, trusts, insurance, and beneficiary designations. Building wealth is protect it so it multiplies across generations and becomes a true inheritance.

5. *Balance Generosity with Growth*

Sending money home is noble, but it must be strategic. Optimize remittances by reducing fees and setting boundaries. At the same time, prioritize investing where you live so your wealth grows, and your giving becomes more sustainable.

Chapter Summary

The immigrant journey begins with courage, the courage to start again. We arrive with more than suitcases. We carry sacrifice, legacy, and hope. The early days often mean starting from the bottom, taking jobs that overlook our skills, pushing through rejection, and learning to balance survival with ambition. Yet those challenges are not wasted. They become training grounds for discipline and persistence, the same qualities that later fuel financial independence.

As this chapter showed, the traits that define immigrants, such as resilience, adaptability, and global perspective, also accelerate wealth-building. The habits of saving, pooling resources, creating multiple income streams, and reinventing ourselves are not new; they are part of how we survive and grow. To reach lasting financial freedom, we must go beyond survival by rewriting the money scripts we inherited, replacing fear with confidence and caution with strategy.

For immigrant women, the climb is often steeper, yet they continue to rise as innovators and builders, turning scarcity into opportunity. Visas and residency shape where and how we create wealth, while remittances remind us that generosity and growth can coexist when managed with intention.

Perhaps the greatest advantage immigrants hold is a bicultural identity that connects two worlds and opens doors others cannot see. Legacy, in the end, is not only about what we leave behind but also about the mindset we pass forward. Through careful planning with wills, trusts, insurance, and investments, we turn effort into impact and move from survival to strength.

Our story is no longer only about endurance. It is a story of freedom, purpose, and transgenerational wealth.

Wealth and Wisdom Declaration

I boldly declare:

I am building wealth and laying a foundation for generations. My labor today becomes legacy tomorrow.

My story will not end with survival; it will resound with significance.

I affirm that my immigrant story is my leverage. What others call struggle, heaven calls strategy.

I was not misplaced; I was planted for purpose.

My journey across borders is proof that grace transcends geography.

I confess that every financial decision I make today shapes my children's tomorrow.

I do not live for momentary gain; I live for eternal impact.

My choices are prophetic seeds, sown into the soil of legacy and destiny.

I decree that I choose to leave wealth, wisdom, and freedom as my inheritance. Not debt, despair, or delay.

The cycle of scarcity breaks with me.

The river of abundance begins and flows through me.

I declare that I am the ancestor my descendants will thank.

My name will be spoken with honor.

My story will be studied as strength.

My footsteps will become roadmaps for generations yet unborn.

I affirm that my resilience, sacrifice, and faith are transforming into abundance that multiplies beyond me.

The walls I break today become the gates my children walk through tomorrow.

The ceilings I shatter become their floors of elevation.

I decree that doors of opportunity open before me because I walk with vision, courage, and divine favor.

Borders do not bind me. Policies cannot limit me. The hand of God advances me.

I confess that I am a bridge-builder between nations; creating wealth across cultures, industries, and generations.

I am a vessel of divine exchange, connecting heaven's wisdom to earthly systems.

My life is proof that purpose prospers anywhere faith is planted.

I declare that lack and scarcity stop with me. Poverty ends in my bloodline. Prosperity begins with my obedience.

I decree that wisdom, wealth, and worship will flow through my lineage without interruption.

I affirm that I am equipped, empowered, and anointed to create transgenerational wealth that honors both my past and my future.

I redeem the sacrifices of those before me.

I resource the destinies of those after me.

I am the convergence of promise and power, grace and grit, faith, and finance.

I am FIRE'D UP to build legacies that outlive time, transcend borders, and testify of God's goodness.

My name will not fade but flourish. My family will not struggle, but we will soar.

My generation will not start from scratch; they will start from strength. Amen.

Disclaimer: This chapter offers education, not legal, tax, or investment advice. Please consult qualified professionals.

Chapter
Nine

TRANSITIONING GRACEFULLY FROM 9-5 TO ENTREPRENEURSHIP

Designing Your Exit with Confidence

I n the last chapter, we explored what it means to design a life of wealth and purpose one that aligns money with your values and vision. The Bedazzled Life by Design™ Framework is about creating a structure where your resources support the life you want to build. But every design eventually reaches the point where it must be lived.

For many high-achieving professionals, that next step means leaving the structure of a 9-to-5. The thought alone can bring both excitement and unease. The steady paycheck, the familiar rhythm, the clear expectations all of it offers comfort. Stepping into entrepreneurship replaces that structure with perceived uncertainty, which can feel intimidating.

That's why this chapter matters. Many people feel anxious about leaving traditional work, not because they lack ability, but because they lack a clear plan or confidence in the one, they have created. This chapter is to help you change that.

You can take intentional steps with wisdom, guided by a plan that turns uncertainty into direction. Now, let's start crafting the transition blueprint for your exit plan.

1. Define Your "Why" and Vision

We've talked throughout this book about the power of purpose how clarity of vision anchors you when everything else feels uncertain. By now, you have likely reflected on what drives you, what matters most, and why you're pursuing financial independence in the first place. Still, it's worth revisiting here, because your why takes on new weight when you start preparing to step away from a paycheck.

For many driven professionals, the first spark doesn't appear in a moment of triumph. It comes on a hard day. You pour yourself into a project, and someone else gets the credit. A promotion goes to a less-experienced colleague. The hours stretch longer, but your paycheck never seems to catch up with your value.

You have climbed the ladder, collected credentials, and proved yourself more times than you can count. Respect may be there. Compensation may be there. Yet something inside you keeps stirring. You've built a life that looks stable from the outside, but something within you keeps asking for more, more meaning, more ownership, more alignment.

That restlessness is not failure; it's a signal. It's your deeper self-asking for work that reflects who you are and what you value. But do not rush to quit just because you feel unfulfilled. Take the time to identify what makes you feel that way. Is it a lack of growth? Lack of freedom? Misalignment with your values? Revisit those questions until you can clearly see what kind of work would allow you to grow, serve, and build around your purpose.

Tony Robbins once said, "If your why is strong enough, the how will reveal itself." Purpose gives clarity to uncertainty. And Proverbs 18:16 reminds us, "Your gift will make room for you and bring you before great men." When you stay aligned with what you were created to do, the right opportunities have a way of meeting you there.

Your why doesn't need to be grand or perfect but it just needs to be true.

Revisit it often.

Write it down.

Let it shape how you move forward from here.

2. Validate Your Business Idea

The dream of entrepreneurship often meets its first wall

at fear. You have worked hard to build credibility in your career, yet the question still lingers: What if I step out, launch this idea I believe in, and no one buys? That fear keeps countless would-be entrepreneurs glued to their cubicles longer than they should be.

The truth is that success in corporate life does not automatically translate into success in the marketplace. Titles, degrees, and certifications may earn respect at work, but customers only respond to value. The only promotion that matters now is when someone says "yes" and is willing to pay. The marketplace has a way of humbling even the most capable professionals.

In Chapter 8, we talked about how to generate and filter Skills to Cash ideas, creative sparks that could evolve into viable businesses. Here, the focus shifts from ideas to evidence. It is no longer about brainstorming possibilities; it's about testing those ideas in the real world while you still have the safety net of your 9-to-5 income.

Validation matters because it keeps you from jumping from certainty into chaos. It gives you a bridge between what you dream and what the market wants. According to CB Insights (2022), 42 percent of failed startups cite "no market need" as the reason for their closure. These weren't untalented or unmotivated founders. They simply built something beautiful that no one needed. Validation keeps you from building that kind of heartbreak.

Here's what that looks like in practice:

Start Small, Start Real

While still employed, create a pilot version of your service or product. Offer it to five to ten real people. Watch what happens. Do they pay, do they engage, do they come back? Their response is more valuable than any survey.

Talk to Your Target Market

A LinkedIn poll, a quick conversation, or even a coffee chat can reveal what a $10,000 market research report might miss. Ask real questions like "What's your biggest frustration with X?" and listen closely. Real problems lead to real opportunities.

Track Willingness, Not Just Interest

People might say they love your idea, but real validation comes when they take action by paying, signing up, or changing a behavior. As Steve Blank, a pioneer of modern entrepreneurship, says, "No facts exist inside the building, only opinions." The truth about your business lives outside your imagination.

Disciplined Testing

Set aside time each week to run small experiments. Your dream won't grow on inspiration alone. Faith without action will keep it on paper instead of in motion.

Adopt this mindset: your 9-to-5 can be the investor that funds your vision and gives you the stability and resources to build something new. That paycheck funds your early tests and protects your household while you learn what works.

As a person of faith, I believe that testing an idea is also another way of discerning God's confirmation and timing. When the time is right, doors open, mentors appear, clients affirm your gifts, and provision meets preparation. What feels like validation in the market is also confirmation in the spirit.

When done well, validation replaces fear with evidence. You no longer must wonder, "What if no one buys?" You'll know, "People are already buying, and now I can build to serve them better." That confidence makes your exit not a gamble, but a step of wisdom.

And as you build this confidence, it's important to remember that your journey doesn't happen in isolation. Your transition will shape the rhythm of your home and the people who share life with you. That's why the next step is just as important: aligning your family with your vision.

3. Align with Your Family

Transitioning from a paycheck to entrepreneurship changes more than your career; it shifts the rhythm of your entire household. When you leave a corporate role, your family leaves it with you. They will feel the long nights, the uncertainty, the tightened budget, and the emotional highs and lows that come with your new chapter. That is why family alignment is essential.

Many professionals try to "protect" their loved ones by keeping their entrepreneurial plans quiet until resignation day. The intention may be good, but silence often creates distance, and distance leads to misunderstanding. Alignment begins with open conversation. Before you resign, sit down with your spouse, children, or closest circle, and talk through what this transition means, what sacrifices might be ahead, and what vision you are all working toward. Invite questions, listen carefully, and show that this is not an impulsive move, but a thoughtful decision made with everyone in mind.

Family alignment also means managing expectations about time. Entrepreneurship can easily spill into every corner of the day if you do not set clear boundaries. Protect family meals, bedtime routines, and milestone events. These are not distractions from your goals; they are part of what gives those goals meaning. Success loses its value when it costs the relationships that matter most.

Research reflects this tension. A Gallup study found that 45 percent of entrepreneurs experience high daily stress, compared to 38 percent of employees. That stress often shows up at home first. But when families are aligned, pressure becomes shared resilience instead of private strain. Your loved ones become your allies, not bystanders. Their encouragement becomes fuel on the days when doubt feels heavy.

When your family is included in the journey, the first paying client becomes a shared victory. The first profitable month is not just your achievement it belongs to everyone who supported you. Your household becomes your first team, your first investors, and your most loyal supporters.

Entrepreneurship will always involve trade-offs, but alignment makes those trade-offs intentional. With alignment, you do not carry the weight alone. You build together, face challenges together, and celebrate progress together.

Once your purpose is clear, your idea validated, and your family aligned, you have the first three pillars of a successful transition. But even with purpose and support, you still need a financial structure to protect your peace of mind. The next step is building your financial runway the cushion that allows you to create boldly without being overwhelmed by uncertainty.

4. Build Your Financial Runway

Your financial runway is the amount of time you can live and operate your business without relying on new income. It acts as a cushion, allowing you to move from employment to entrepreneurship without panic-driven decisions. The longer your runway, the smoother and more confident your transition becomes.

Most businesses do not become profitable overnight. A U.S. Bank study found that 82 percent of small businesses fail due to poor cash flow management. SCORE (2023) reports that the average small business takes 2 to 3 years to reach steady profitability. Leaving a paycheck without a solid cushion can create unnecessary stress or even force an early return to the very job you hoped to leave behind.

How to Build Your Runway While Employed

1. Calculate Your Burn Rate

Add up your monthly living expenses, such as housing, food, utilities, debt payments, and insurance, along with projected startup costs like software, marketing, and supplies. This total is your burn rate.

Example: If your family requires $4,000 per month and your startup adds $1,000, your burn rate is $5,000.

2. Multiply for Security

Aim for 12 to 18 months of expenses saved in liquid, conservative accounts before resigning. Using the example above, your target runway would be between $60,000 and $90,000. This margin of safety allows you to breathe while your business finds its footing.

3. Choose the Right Vehicles

- **_High-Yield Savings Accounts (HYSAs):_** Keep funds accessible while earning interest.

- **_Treasury Bills or Money Market Accounts:_** Low-risk, short-term options that preserve capital.

- **Separate Business Account:** Keep your business runway distinct from household accounts. Clear separation provides peace of mind and accurate tracking.

4. Trim and Reallocate

Use your 9-to-5 income to save intentionally. Automate transfers, reduce unnecessary spending, and redirect those funds toward your runway. Every dollar you save strengthens your ability to build freely later.

5. Treat Side-Hustle Income as Bonus Runway

View any side-hustle income as additional runway, not extra spending money. It may be tempting to reward yourself early, but discipline now creates flexibility later.

Building your runway is not a sign of hesitation. Preparation is wisdom in action. When your financial foundation is secure, you can create with confidence rather than react out of fear. Your runway also buys you time to learn. The early months of entrepreneurship will involve trial and error—testing offers, refining pricing, and discovering your market rhythm.

With 12 to 18 months of savings in place, you can experiment without the pressure of "I have to make this work immediately." Panic creates short-sighted decisions. Preparation builds long-term stability.

> *"Runway is just velocity in disguise."*
>
> *Naval Ravikant*

In other words, the more financial space you give yourself, the faster and farther you can move. A long runway doesn't just keep you safe but also gives you momentum. It gives you time to make smarter choices, refine your offers, and grow at a healthy pace rather than rushing for survival. With your runway in place, you have created both protection and momentum. But financial preparation is only one part of a strong transition.

Structuring for Success (Global Lens)

Your business cannot thrive on passion alone. It needs structure the kind that keeps you steady when growth brings complexity. Before you hand in your resignation, make sure the foundation you have built can carry the weight of your next season.

Earlier in this book, we covered the importance of establishing your business legally and financially choosing an entity type, setting up accounts, and protecting your intellectual property. This section brings those ideas together as a final readiness check before you transition. The goal is to ensure the essentials are in place and functioning smoothly.

Core Steps for Professionals Transitioning (U.S. Context)

1. *Legal Entity*

Register your business as a Limited Liability Company (LLC) or an S-Corporation, depending on your goals and tax profile. This creates a legal separation between your personal and business finances, protecting your assets and potentially reducing your tax burden as you scale.

2. *EIN (Employer Identification Number)*

Apply for an EIN through the IRS website. It's free and functions like a Social Security Number for your business. You'll need it to open bank accounts, file taxes, and sign contracts.

3. *Business Banking*

Open a dedicated business checking account before you begin accepting payments. Keeping finances separate avoids confusion, builds credibility, and makes tax preparation far easier.

4. *Accounting System*

Set up bookkeeping software such as QuickBooks, Wave, or Xero early on. Even if your first transactions are small, good recordkeeping prevents stress later and gives you a clear picture of cash flow from day one.

5. *Contracts and Policies*

Create basic service agreements, non-disclosure forms,

and refund or cancellation policies. You don't need a law degree to start—use clear, simple language and update your templates as your business grows. Clarity builds trust with clients and protects your work.

6. *Intellectual Property and Data Privacy*

Avoid using materials developed under your current employer's ownership. Register your business name, claim your domain, and implement simple data protection practices if you collect client information. These steps show foresight and professionalism.

7. *Insurance and Risk Protection*

Consider professional liability insurance or general business coverage once you begin accepting clients. These policies can protect you from unexpected claims and help you present yourself as a serious, prepared business owner.

Think of this checklist as baby-proofing your business. Each step may seem small, but together they create a stable foundation that allows you to scale.

A Global Perspective

Because this book serves readers across borders, it is important to recognize that every country has its own version of these systems. The table below offers a quick reference guide to the foundational structures you will encounter in different regions.

A Global Perspective

Topic	United States	United Kingdom	Canada	Nigeria	India
Entity (starter)	LLC/S Corp	Limited Company /Sole Trader	Corporation / Sole Proprietorship	CAC Business Name - Ltd	Private Limited / LLP
Tax ID	EIN	UTR + Company Number	BN (Business Number)	CAC Number	PAN + CIN
Health Coverage	COBRA/ACA	NHS + Private Plans	Provincial Plans + Private	HMO / Private Plans	Private Plans
Retirement (solo)	Solo 401(k) /SEP-IRA	SIPP	RRSP / IPP	Pension funds / Private Schemes	NPS / PPF
Sales Tax / VAT	State-based Sales Tax	VAT	GST / HST	VAT	GST

Wherever you are, formal structure shows commitment. Register your business, secure your tax ID, and put proper systems in place. These steps are more than administration; they show that you take your work seriously and are prepared to build something that lasts.

Now the question is how to move from employee to entrepreneur without panic or haste. For many, the answer lies in a phased transition.

Phased Transition to Entrepreneurship

Not every exit has to be sudden or dramatic. Most successful entrepreneurs begin with a phased transition, balancing the stability of their paycheck with the gradual build of their business. This approach reduces financial pressure and builds confidence because you are learning while your household needs are still being met.

A 2021 Global Entrepreneurship Monitor study found that 65 percent of entrepreneurs worldwide start their businesses while still employed. This pattern holds across the United States, Nigeria, Canada, and much of the diaspora. Many professionals test their ideas in the evenings or on weekends before fully stepping out. The principle remains the same across regions: transition in stages, not in panic.

The Phased Pathway

A thoughtful transition usually happens in stages, each building on the last.

1. *The Side Hustle Phase*

This is where you begin testing your business idea while still employed. You might start consulting, freelancing, selling a product online, or offering small workshops. Your paycheck becomes the investor that funds your early experiments without putting your household at risk.

2. *The Part-Time Shift*

Once you gain traction, the next step may be reducing hours, negotiating remote work, or creating a consulting arrangement with your employer. Many companies are willing to retain your expertise in a smaller capacity rather than lose you entirely. This setup maintains income stability while freeing time to grow your venture.

3. *The Full Transition*

The final stage comes when your side hustle consistently covers at least half of your household expenses, and your financial runway is secure. At this point, you are not jumping into uncertainty you are stepping onto a bridge you've already tested.

Consider the story of an immigrant engineer in Texas who moved from full-time employment to a 20-hour-per-week consulting role with her former company. That part-time paycheck served as her safety net while she built her engineering services firm. Within a year, her business earned more than her old salary. She transitioned fully without panic, without debt, and without damaged relationships.

Across Africa, the trend is similar. A 2022 Jobberman survey found that more than 40 percent of Nigerian professionals run side businesses alongside their main jobs. Many begin by registering a Business Name with the Corporate Affairs Commission, operate evenings and weekends, and then formalize as Limited Liability Companies once revenue grows. In Canada, professionals often start as sole proprietors before incorporating, and in the United Kingdom, many begin as sole traders before forming Limited Companies.

Resignation Logistics

Phasing out of employment is about more than timing. It's also about how you leave. A well-handled resignation becomes both a professional milestone and a bridge to future opportunities. A careless one can harm your reputation and make your transition harder than it needs to be.

1. *Notice Period*

Honor your company's policy by giving proper notice usually two to four weeks, though leadership roles may require more. Your last impression carries as much weight as your first. Leave with professionalism and gratitude to protect your reputation and references.

2. Handover and Documentation

Prepare clear handover notes for your team or successor. Include ongoing projects, contacts, and key deadlines. This shows maturity and reliability, and it keeps your professional relationships intact if collaboration becomes possible later.

3. References and Relationships

Stay connected. Request written or verbal references from managers and peers who value your work. Many new entrepreneurs find that their first clients or referrals come from these very networks.

4. Update Your Professional Presence

Refresh your LinkedIn profile, résumé, and personal website to reflect your new chapter. Frame it as growth, not departure. For example:

"After ten years in corporate finance, I now help organizations and individuals accelerate wealth growth through [your service]." The way you describe your transition shapes how others perceive your new identity.

5. Manage Benefits and Retirement Accounts

Before resigning, review your health coverage options, roll over any retirement accounts, and confirm that life insurance remains active. Overlooking these details can cause costly gaps in your safety net. Protecting these assets is part of your financial runway.

6. *Confidentiality and Non-Competes*

If your role involves intellectual property or a non-compete clause, consult a lawyer before you resign. Make sure you understand what you can and cannot do as you start your business. Upholding integrity here safeguards both your reputation and your future work.

Network Activation: The Hidden Multiplier

When most people think of networking, they picture exchanging business cards, sending LinkedIn requests, or reciting an elevator pitch. But as you transition from employee to entrepreneur, your network becomes much more than a list of names. It becomes the bridge between your paycheck world and your purpose-driven future.

Opportunities rarely appear in isolation. They flow through people. Yet many professionals make the mistake of keeping their entrepreneurial ambitions hidden until the day they resign, fearing judgment or misunderstanding. That silence often closes the very doors that could have helped refine or accelerate their ideas.

Strategic activation looks different. It is less about collecting contacts and more about cultivating genuine conversations. Share your early concepts with trusted peers, alumni groups, or mastermind circles. Keep it simple and honest. "I'm testing a solution for this problem. Can

I get your feedback?" Each conversation helps you clarify your message and sharpen your offer.

Your network can also serve as a feedback loop. Before a formal launch, test early versions of your product or service with people you trust. If they buy, commit, or refer you, that is proof that your idea has traction. Sometimes the most valuable connections will come from unexpected places a friend from church, a neighbor, or someone who believes in your vision.

Approach every connection with generosity. Offer advice, share insights, or introduce others before asking for anything in return. Relationships built on genuine values tend to grow into long-term partnerships that support your journey.

Invite people into your story. Let them see your progress, lessons, and milestones along the way. People are drawn to authenticity and are more likely to support what they feel connected to. A Harvard Business Review study found that 84 percent of entrepreneurs gained their first customers through personal and professional networks. Your paycheck may provide stability today, but your network will create the opportunities that will sustain you tomorrow. Nurture it with care and consistency, and it will help carry your vision further than effort alone ever could.

Your network helps you open doors, but relationships alone will not sustain your progress. Once opportunities begin to grow, structure becomes essential. Systems, routines, and accountability keep you steady when life gets full and distractions multiply. This next section will help you design rhythms that protect your time, your focus, and the vision you are building.

Systems, Routines, and Accountability

Leaving corporate life means leaving behind the structure that once guided your days. Meetings, deadlines, and managers provided order. In entrepreneurship, that structure disappears unless you build it yourself.

The habits you create, how you plan, prioritize, and hold yourself accountable, become the framework that protects your time and energy. Systems and routines are how you honor your goals and make progress possible.

1. Design your days with intention.

Start each morning with grounding habits such as prayer, movement, or journaling to prepare your mind and body. Block time for deep work before distractions appear, and close each day by protecting family time, rest, and renewal. Treat your calendar as a plan for your energy, not just a record of tasks.

2. Create a simple system for leads and clients.

In entrepreneurship, consistent income depends on consistent follow-up. Use a spreadsheet or a Customer Relationship Management (CRM) tool to track contacts, conversations, and next steps. Review your pipeline weekly so potential opportunities never go unnoticed.

3. **Schedule a weekly money review.**

Set aside a consistent time each week to review income, expenses, and savings for tax purposes. Whether you use software or a basic ledger, this practice keeps your finances clear and prevents surprises. Clarity builds confidence and allows you to make decisions based on facts, not fear.

4. **Build accountability into your growth.**

Replace the built-in structure of corporate life with a supportive circle. A mentor offers guidance rooted in experience. A mastermind group provides peers who challenge and encourage you. A coach helps you identify blind spots and refine your strategy. Accountability keeps progress steady when motivation fades.

Together, these systems form the scaffolding for your next chapter. They give rhythm to your days, clarity to your finances, and structure to your goals. Freedom without discipline creates chaos. Freedom supported by structure creates sustainability.

The 30-60-90 Day Transition Map

We've learned the pieces: validation, structure, and activation. What follows is a suggested 90-day rhythm for putting them in motion. This map brings everything together into a clear sequence, helping you move from preparation to confident action without feeling overwhelmed.

The 30–60–90 Day Transition Map

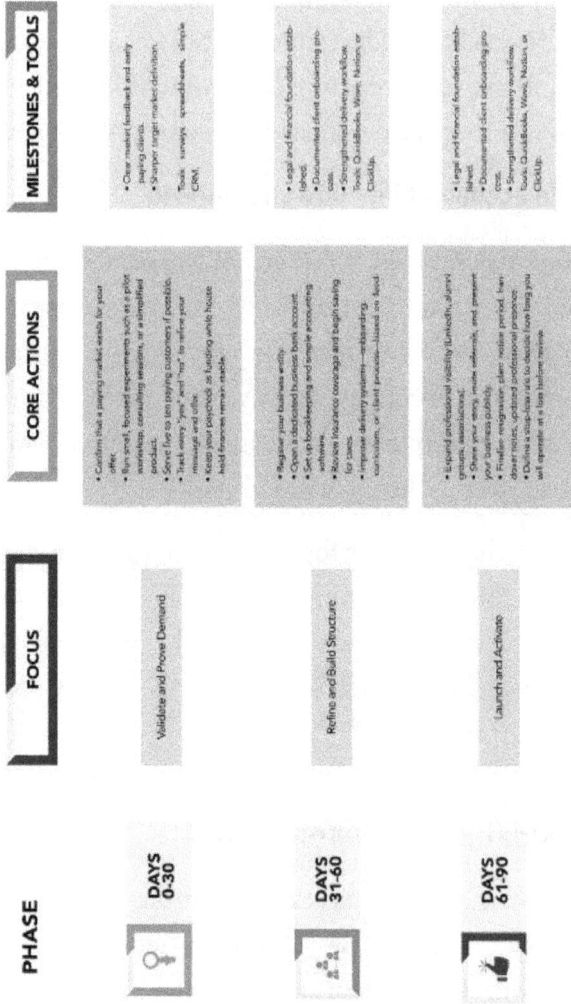

PHASE	FOCUS	CORE ACTIONS	MILESTONES & TOOLS
DAYS 0-30	Validate and Prove Demand	• Confirm that a paying market exists for your offer. • Run small, focused experiments such as a pilot workshop, consulting sessions, or a simplified product. • Serve five to ten paying customers if possible. • Track every "yes" and "no" to refine your message and offer. • Keep your paycheck as funding while house-hold finances remain stable.	• Clear market feedback and early paying clients. • Sharper target market definition. Tools: surveys, spreadsheets, simple CRM.
DAYS 31-60	Refine and Build Structure	• Register your business entity. • Open a dedicated business bank account. • Set up bookkeeping and simple accounting software. • Review insurance coverage and begin saving for taxes. • Improve delivery systems—onboarding, curriculum, or client process—based on feedback.	• Legal and financial foundation established. • Documented client onboarding process. • Strengthened delivery workflow. Tools: QuickBooks, Wave, Notion, or ClickUp.
DAYS 61-90	Launch and Activate	• Expand professional visibility (LinkedIn, alumni groups, associations). • Share your story, case referrals, and present your business publicly. • Finalize resignation plans: notice period, handover notes, updated professional proposal. • Define a side-by-run schedule so you know how long you can operate at a loss before review.	• Legal and financial foundation established. • Documented client onboarding process. • Strengthened delivery workflow. Tools: QuickBooks, Wave, Notion, or ClickUp.

Wealthness™: Protecting the Asset Called You

Earlier in this book, we explored the concept of Wealthness™, the discipline of managing both your money and your mind with intention. As you move toward your 9–5 exit, this practice becomes even more important. The foundation you are building depends on your clarity, focus, and health.

Gallup's State of the Global Workplace Report (2023) says, 44 percent of employees said they experienced significant stress the previous day. Entrepreneurs often face even higher levels of daily pressure. Chronic stress, poor sleep, and neglect of health weaken the body and cloud judgment. The American Institute of Stress estimates that workplace stress costs U.S. businesses over $300 billion each year in lost productivity, medical bills, and turnover.

Wealthness™ in this season means protecting the asset called you.

Core Practices of Wealthness™

Rest as Strategy

Sleep is not wasted time; it is the body's reset button. Studies from the CDC show that adults who consistently sleep fewer than six hours per night are at higher risk of heart disease, obesity, and reduced cognitive function. Rest restores the energy needed to lead well.

Move for Clarity

Exercise isn't only about physique. It sharpens focus, releases stress, and improves creativity. Even a 30-minute daily walk can increase problem-solving capacity by 60 percent. Nourish for Energy. Food is fuel. Entrepreneurs who rely on processed sugar and caffeine crashes often find their performance follows the same peaks and valleys. Whole, nutrient-dense foods sustain energy and resilience.

Mental Fitness

Journaling, meditation, or prayer-centered reflection equip you to manage uncertainty without being consumed by it. Protecting your mind is as essential as protecting your body.

Boundaries

One of the hidden dangers of entrepreneurship is overwork. Without the structure of corporate office hours, the lines blur. Establishing boundaries for work, family, and rest protects both your health and your relationships.

Caring for your health is part of your transition plan. A clear mind and strong body give you the endurance to lead, build, and create with excellence as you design your next chapter. Protecting yourself is not separate from work. It is part of building something that lasts.

Chapter Summary

Transitioning gracefully from corporate life to entrepreneurship is not a single leap but a carefully designed journey. In this chapter, we walked through what it means to leave the security of a paycheck with wisdom, step into purpose with clarity, and prepare yourself and the people who matter most for the new rhythm ahead.

It begins with courage, but not reckless courage. Defining your "why" anchors you when challenges come. Validating your business idea helps ensure you are solving a problem people are willing to pay for. Bringing your family along in the process turns private dreams into shared resilience. With those foundations in place, you are no longer chasing an idea; you are building something that lasts.

Preparation also means getting practical. A solid financial runway protects your creativity from panic and pressure. Putting the right legal, financial, and operational systems in place sets you up for real growth. Transitioning in phases, from side hustle to part-time to full-time entrepreneurship, gives you time to test, learn, and strengthen before taking the full step. Resigning with care, leaving clear documentation and strong relationships behind, allows you to move forward without closing important doors.

Mindset shapes everything that follows. Resilience, adaptability, and a willingness to keep learning matter as much as any business plan. Practicing Wealthness™ protecting your rest, health, and clarity keeps you capable of leading well. Family rhythms and boundaries remind you why you started. Activating your network with honesty and generosity opens doors you could never force on your own.

Systems and accountability hold everything together. Daily habits, thoughtful calendar design, lead tracking, regular financial check-ins, and trusted mentors turn freedom into focus. The 30-60-90 Day Transition Map helps you put these pieces into motion, guiding you through testing, refining, and launching with confidence and calm.

People often say that the biggest risk is not taking any. Transitioning from employment to entrepreneurship is not about walking away from security. It is about building a different kind of stability, one grounded in preparation, vision, and courage. With wisdom and faith, you do not just leave a job; you step into a season where your gifts, skills, and passion create value on your own terms.

Wealth and Wisdom Declaration

"Commit to the Lord whatever you do, and He will establish your plans."— *Proverbs 16:3*

I boldly declare:

I decree that my transition from paycheck to purpose is covered with wisdom, favor, and divine alignment.

I move with peace, not panic; strategy, not struggle; and purpose, not pressure.

I declare that every step I take; whether validating my idea, building my runway, or launching my business ushers me into greater abundance.

Each task is a seed; each risk is a revelation; each act of faith is a foundation for fortune.

I confess that my gifts make room for me and open doors of opportunity before great men and women.

My creativity is currency, and my competence is covenant.

I no longer hide behind titles; I rise as the visionary CEO of my calling.

I affirm that lack, fear, and scarcity no longer have power over me.

I walk boldly in faith, stewardship, and creativity.

The same God who prospered me in employment prospers me in enterprise.

I am not leaving safety; I am entering significance.

I declare that my family is aligned with my vision.

We build a legacy of abundance and generational wealth.

Unity is our superpower, and peace is our prosperity.

I decree that my health, energy, and clarity are preserved.

My body is the engine of divine purpose and prosperity.

I rest without guilt, rise with focus, and work from overflow, not exhaustion.

I decree that my network is activated with divine connections; mentors, strategic alliances, partners, clients, crusaders, and collaborators who accelerate my impact.

Heaven orchestrates introductions. Destiny relationships locate me without delay.

I declare that I have the discipline to follow through, the resilience to overcome setbacks, and the faith to see abundance manifest.

I do not quit; I recalibrate. I do not retreat; I reinvent.

Every obstacle becomes an opportunity for elevation.

I confess that my systems, routines, processes, and strategies are blessed and fruitful.

What I build prospers. What I launch lasts. My efforts multiply with supernatural increase.

I affirm that my transition is not just a career change, but it is a calling fulfilled.

I step into this new season with courage, abundance, and unshakable faith.

I am not losing stability; I am gaining sovereignty.

I am not leaving employment; I am entering empowerment.

I decree that I am FIRE'D UP to build, lead, and prosper in purpose.

I am a pioneer of possibility, a vessel of vision, and a steward of supernatural success.

My transition is graceful, my growth is guaranteed, and my glory is God-ordained. Amen.

Chapter
Ten

BUILDING THE FIRE READINESS ASSESSMENT & JOINING THE MOVEMENT

You have walked with me through ideas and tools that challenge the old way of living. We began by breaking free from scarcity and shifting from paycheck dependence to possibility. We explored how money becomes more powerful when it is aligned with meaning rather than control. We saw that freedom is built from choices to diversify income, master systems, grow wisely, and design life with purpose.

Now, it is time to pause.

Think of this chapter as a mirror. The FIRE Readiness Assessment is your scorecard not a verdict or a judgment, but a checkpoint. It shows you where you stand today and the fastest ways to move forward. Just like an annual health checkup reveals whether your heart is strong, or your blood pressure needs attention, this financial checkup reveals the strength of your foundations and where you may still be vulnerable.

Awareness shortens timelines. Seeing where you're vulnerable makes it easier to take practical steps forward. When you know your strengths, you can build on them. This is how professionals who once believed financial independence was decades away realize they can accelerate their timeline by years.

This assessment is built on the four pillars we have explored throughout this book:

- Income Diversification (Make Money)

- Money Mastery Systems (Manage Money)

- Wealth Growth & Protection (Multiply & Protect)

- Life & Wealth Design (Money with Meaning)

Each pillar contains a few non-negotiable questions designed to get to the heart of your financial readiness. Answer honestly, and in about ten minutes you'll know whether you are a Starter, Builder, Accelerator, or Trailblazer.

Why FIRE Matters & Why Take the Assessment

FIRE (Financial Independence, Retire Early) is not about quitting work or sitting on a beach for the rest of your life. It's about freedom. Freedom to choose work you love, to spend time with people who matter, to do work that brings fulfillment, and to live in alignment with your values.

But here's the challenge: too many professionals confuse stability with security. A paycheck feels safe until it isn't. A promotion feels like progress until you realize it keeps you stuck longer. FIRE reframes the goal: not just surviving on income but designing a life where your money works for you, not the other way around.

The assessment tells you the truth the distance between "paycheck dependence" and "financial independence." It helps you see your current position clearly and plan your next steps with confidence.

By taking this quick test, you'll:

● See where you fall: Starter, Builder, Accelerator, or Trailblazer.

● Understand your "Must Fix" areas the red flags that, when addressed, collapse timelines.

● Gain clarity on how many years you are truly away from FIRE and not just in theory, but in practice.

The FIRE Readiness Mini-Assessment This assessment is short, simple, and powerful. It's designed to give you an honest snapshot of where you are on your FIRE journey today.

Instructions: Circle the answer that best fits you.

- Each question scores 1–5 points.

- 1 = weakest (Must Fix = urgent gap), 5 = strongest.

- Add your pillar totals, then your grand total (out of 80).

Pillar 1: Income Diversification (Make Money)

Q1. How much of your income comes from a single paycheck?

1 = All (Must Fix)

2 = 70–80%

3 = 50–69%

4 = 30–49%

5 = Less than 30%

Q2. How many distinct income streams do you currently have?

1 = None (Must Fix)

2 = 1

3 = 2

4 = 3–4

5 = 5+

Q3. Do you earn money even when you're not actively working (passive income)?

1 = None (Must Fix)

2 = Very little

3 = Some

4 = Moderate

5 = Significant

Q4. If you lost your job today, what's your fallback income source?

1 = None (Must Fix)

2 = Savings only

3 = Side hustle

4 = Rental income

5 = Established business

Subtotal (Pillar 1 Score out of 20): _____

Pillar 2: Money Mastery Systems (Manage Money)

Q5. Do you track your income and expenses monthly?

1 = No (Must Fix)

2 = Rarely

3 = Sometimes

4 = Most months

5 = Every month without fail

Q6. Do you have 3–6 months of living expenses saved in an emergency fund?

1 = No (Must Fix)

2 = 1 month saved

3 = 2–3 months saved

4 = 4–5 months saved

5 = 6+ months saved

Q7. Do you carry high-interest debt (credit cards, payday loans)?

1 = Yes, significant (Must Fix)

2 = Yes, moderate

3 = Somewhat manageable

4 = Very little, low-interest only

5 = None

Q8. Could you cover a $5,000 emergency tomorrow

without borrowing?

1 = Not at all (Must Fix)

2 = $1–2K available

3 = Could cover most but not all

4 = Yes, with effort

5 = Yes, easily

Subtotal (Pillar 2 Score out of 20): _____

Pillar 3: Wealth Growth & Protection (Multiply & Protect Money)

Q9. Are your investments on track to replace your salary in 10 years or less?

1 = Nowhere close (Must Fix)

2 = 15–20 years away

3 = 10–15 years away

4 = 5–10 years away

5 = Less than 5 years away

Q10. Do you understand how your money is invested and how it grows?

1 = No idea (Must Fix)

2 = Very little understanding

3 = Somewhat understand

4 = Mostly understand

5 = Fully confident and informed

Q11. Is your portfolio diversified enough to survive an economic downturn?

1 = Not at all (Must Fix)

2 = Slightly diversified

3 = Moderately diversified

4 = Well-diversified

5 = Fully hedged/diversified

Q12. If you passed away tomorrow, would your family be financially secure?

1 = Severe risk (Must Fix)

2 = Some risk

3 = Moderately secure

4 = Secure

5 = Fully protected

Subtotal (Pillar 3 Score out of 20): _____

Q13. Have you defined your ideal lifestyle and calculated its cost?

1 = Not at all (Must Fix)

2 = Only thought about it

3 = Rough idea

4 = Detailed but not updated

5 = Fully defined and updated

Q14. Do you have a clear, written FIRE vision and target age?

1 = None (Must Fix)

2 = Vague idea

3 = Somewhat clear

4 = Clear and written down

5 = Fully actionable

Q15. If you reached FIRE tomorrow, how clear is your life's purpose?

1 = None

2 = Vague

3 = Somewhat clear

4 = Mostly clear

5 = Very clear

Q16. Are you building a financial story that leads to freedom or regret?

1 = Heading toward regret (Must Fix)

2 = Some regret

3 = Mixed trajectory

4 = Mostly toward freedom

5 = Fully toward freedom

Subtotal (Pillar 4 Score out of 20): _____

Grand Total

Add all pillar subtotals (out of 80): _____

Remember: the total is important, but the Must Fix flags are even more important. You can have a decent overall score, but if you're still paycheck-dependent, carrying high-interest debt, or missing an emergency fund, your entire foundation is fragile.

"Your score is not your sentence. It's your starting line." — *Lola Wealth*

Your FIRE Readiness Scorecard

Step 1: Add up your answers for each pillar (max = 20).

Step 2: Add all four pillars for your total score (max = 80).

Step 3: Match your total to your FIRE Identity below.

Pillar Breakdown

Pillar	Your Score (out of 20)	Readiness Level
Income Diversification (Make Money)	___ / 20	Weak / Developing / Strong / Mastery
Money Mastery Systems (Manage Money)	___ / 20	Weak / Developing / Strong / Mastery
Wealth Growth & Protection (Multiply & Protect)	___ / 20	Weak / Developing / Strong / Mastery
Life & Wealth Design (Money with Meaning)	___ / 20	Weak / Developing / Strong / Mastery

Your FIRE Identity

Total Score (out of 80)	FIRE Identity	Projected Years to FIRE
0–29	Starter	15–20 years
30–44	Builder	10–15 years
45–59	Accelerator	5–10 years
60–80	Trailblazer	3–5 years

Your FIRE Roadmap

Step 1: Score Your Readiness

From the 16-question assessment, total your score out of 80:

Starter (0–29) Paycheck dependent, 15–20 years from FIRE

Builder (30–44) Early momentum, 10–15 years from FIRE

Accelerator (45–59) Strong systems, 5–10 years from FIRE

Trailblazer (60–80) Mastery, 3–5 years from FIRE

Red Flags (Must Fix): If you circled any 1s (no emergency fund, paycheck dependence, high-interest debt, no protection, no vision), fix those first because they can collapse years off your timeline.

Step 2: Calculate Your FIRE Number

This is your Financial Independence (FI) Target:

Formula:

Annual Spending × 25 = FIRE Number

Gap = FIRE Number – Current Savings/Investments

Years to FIRE = Gap ÷ Annual Savings

Example:

Annual Spending × 25 = FIRE Number

- Annual Spending = $50,000

- FIRE Number = $1,250,000

Find Your Gap

Formula:

FIRE Number − Current Savings/Investments = Gap

- FIRE Number = $1,250,000

- Current Net Worth = $250,000

- Gap = $1,000,000

Estimate Your Years to FIRE

Formula:

Gap ÷ Annual Savings = Years to FIRE

- Gap = $1,000,000

- Annual Savings = $50,000

- Years to FIRE ≈ 20 years

Roadmap at a Glance

State	Score Range	Typical FIRE Horizon	Next Levers to Collapse Time
Starter	0–29	15–20 years	1. Build $1,000 cushion. 2. Start 1 additional income stream. 3. Hit 20% savings rate.
Builder	30–44	10–15 years	1. Grow emergency funds for 3–6 months. 2. Raise savings rate to 30–40%. 3. Add 1 passive income stream.
Accelerator	45–59	5–10 years	1. Hit 40–50% savings rate. 2. Diversify portfolio across 3+ assets. 3. Optimize taxes + reinvest all side income.
Trailblazer	60–80	3–5 years	1. Protect wealth (insurance, trusts). 2. Focus on legacy + impact. 3. Expand scalable income streams.

Your FIRE Roadmap = Identity + Number.

● Your Score (out of 80) shows where you stand today.

● Your FIRE Number shows the wealth target you need.

● Your Gap ÷ Savings shows how long it takes at your current pace.

● Your Next Levers show how to collapse decades into years.

If you're ready to go deeper, scan the second QR code to take the Full FIRE Readiness Assessment. It's a more detailed diagnostic that builds on the mini assessment in this chapter, giving you a more personalized roadmap to shorten your timeline and strengthen your foundations.

Because this moment is more than a score, it's the beginning of a story — your story of freedom, faith, and fulfillment.

"Freedom is not someday. Freedom is a decision. And today is the day you choose it." — Lola Wealth

Join the Movement: The FIRE'D UP Collective™

As a driven professional, you were not created to work for decades only to retire exhausted.

You have journeyed through this book, asked yourself honest questions, and seen where you stand. That awareness is powerful, but awareness alone isn't enough. Freedom begins when you take the next step, and when you take it with others who share your vision.

The old model of life; study hard, climb the corporate ladder, wait for a pension, and hope to enjoy what is left at 65, no longer works. Many of us have watched our parents, mentors, and colleagues give their best years to work, only to retire weary and unfulfilled.

The FIRE'D UP Collective was created to change that story. It is a community of professionals, entrepreneurs, and dreamers who are ready to live differently, to build lives where money supports purpose, joy, and legacy.

This movement is not about doing nothing. It is about reclaiming your time, energy, and choices so you can do work that matters. Work that reflects your values. Work that brings fulfillment. True wealth lies in the freedom to choose how you live and serve.

Inside the community, you will meet people who understand the road you are on because they are walking it too. Some are just beginning. Others are further along. All are committed to helping one another grow.

Here, you will gain clarity from proven strategies, encouragement when progress feels slow, and accountability to keep going when life gets busy. You will find mentors who have already accelerated their own journey and peers who remind you that you are not alone.

Most of all, you will belong to a community that believes freedom is not a dream to chase later. It is a life you can design now.

Join us at **FIREdUpCollective.com** or scan the QR code in this chapter to take your next step.

What You Gain in the Collective

Without Community (Paycheck Trap)

○ You rely on one paycheck, always one layoff away from panic.

○ You guess at financial moves, hoping you're on the right path.

○ You carry stress and fear in silence.

○ You feel isolated — friends and colleagues don't understand your FIRE goals.

○ You lose years to hesitation, distraction, or starting over.

○ You chase money without purpose, risking regret at the end.

Inside the FIRE'D UP Collective

○ You design multiple income streams with guidance and proven models.

○ You gain clarity from assessments, roadmaps, and tailored coaching.

○ You gain accountability, encouragement, and people walking the same road.

○ You find belonging with professionals and visionaries who "get it."

○ You collapse decades into years with mentorship and collective momentum.

○ You align wealth with purpose, building joy, freedom, and legacy.

Who This Community is for:

This isn't for the already comfortable or the endlessly theoretical. The Collective is for you if:

- You're tired of living paycheck to paycheck, with your whole future tied to one employer.

- You work harder each year but feel like you're never truly getting ahead.

- Debt, bills, and financial stress make freedom feel out of reach.

- You're an immigrant or diaspora professional who left your home country for better opportunities but refuse to wait decades to enjoy the life you envisioned.

- You're a mid-career professional who has hit the glass ceiling and promotions stall, growth slows, and you know your potential is bigger than your paycheck.

- You're a woman in corporate, balancing ambition, office politics, bias, and family, determined to create wealth on your own terms.

- You're a professional in corporate who wants to retire earlier than 65, not to stop working, but to design life around purpose and choice.

- You've tasted success, the title, the promotion, the house but deep down you know true freedom is still far away.

- If any of this sounds like you, you belong here. Join us!

Why Now?

Every year you wait, you trade away the most valuable resource you have time. The FIRE'D UP Collective is your chance to stop drifting and start designing. It is an opportunity to move from planning to living, from waiting for "someday" to building freedom today.

This movement is about more than money. It is about legacy. It is about the stories your children and grandchildren will one day talk about, how you chose to live. It is about creating a future where you are financially, spiritually, mentally, and emotionally free.

This is your invitation to join a community that believes retirement does not begin at 65. It begins the moment you decide to live free.

Assessments bring awareness, but transformation happens in community. When you surround yourself with people who share your vision, you grow faster and stay grounded. You find encouragement, wisdom, and accountability from those who are building the same kind of freedom you seek. This is about creating legacy and living in a way that shapes the generations that follow. Freedom begins when you choose it.

"Your FIRE journey is measurable, not magical."

— Lola Wealth

Action Steps

This is your turning point. You've faced the truth, seen your score, and identified your "Must Fix" areas. Now it's time to step into a movement that ensures you never walk alone.

Join the **FIRE'D UP Collective™** today.

Step into freedom, faith, and fulfillment, today.

Scan the QR code in this chapter or visit https://www.firedupmovement.com/ to:

- ● Take the full FIRE Readiness Assessment online and get w.lolawealth.com/schedule

Chapter Summary

In this chapter, you measured your readiness with the FIRE Mini-Assessment and gained clarity across the four essential pillars: Income Diversification, Money Mastery Systems, Wealth Growth and Protection, and Life and Wealth Design. You saw how addressing "must-fix" red flags can shorten your timeline to freedom and how your total score reflects both your FIRE identity and your path ahead.

But this chapter was about more than numbers. It was an invitation into the FIRE'D UP Collective, a global movement of professionals who are rewriting what retirement looks like and choosing freedom now instead of waiting for someday. The assessment served as a mirror, giving you an honest picture of where you stand. The community offers acceleration, accountability, and support as you move forward. Together, they form a roadmap to a life rooted in freedom, faith, and fulfillment.

Even though you have reached the end of this book, your journey is just beginning. The FIRE Readiness Assessment showed you where you are today. The FIRE'D UP Collective extends its hand to walk with you toward what is next. Whether you are a Starter, Builder, Accelerator, or Trailblazer, your path is clear: stay aware, make bold choices, and surround yourself with community.

This journey has always been about freedom. It is about living with intention instead of defaulting to routine. It is about pursuing your purpose, investing in what matters, and creating a legacy that will last for generations.

The greatest mistake is not starting late but never starting at all. By reading, reflecting, and taking action, you have already taken the most important step.

Wealth and Wisdom Declaration

"The Lord will open to you His good treasure, the heavens, to bless all the work of your hands."— Deuteronomy 28:12

I boldly declare:

I am a steward of abundance, entrusted by God to build wealth with wisdom and purpose.

I handle money with maturity, manage resources with revelation, and multiply value with vision.

I affirm that I am free from paycheck dependence.

I am no longer confined by the limits of a single income or the boundaries of a job description.

I step boldly into financial freedom; designing, creating, and commanding wealth with divine strategy.

I declare that my income is growing, diversifying, and multiplying through divine doors of opportunity.

New streams open for me with ease.

I am surrounded by favor, guided by insight, and propelled by divine momentum.

I affirm that I master money with discipline, clarity, and faith and money no longer masters me.

I lead my finances with wisdom and rest in God's provision with peace.

I live by divine design, not by financial pressure.

I declare that my wealth is protected, resilient, and aligned with God's promises for my future.

What I build will not break. What I plant will not perish.

My legacy is shielded by divine insurance and multiplied by grace.

I decree that I am creating a financial story of freedom, fulfillment, and generational impact.

My testimony will ignite nations, my story will empower generations, and my results will glorify God.

I declare that I attract divine connections, mentors, and opportunities that accelerate my journey to FIRE.

Strategic allies locate me. Kingdom financiers invest in me. Heavenly helpers advance me.

I affirm that my wealth is purpose-driven, aligned with my values, and fueled by vision.

I prosper with purity, I rise with responsibility, and I give with gratitude.

Every blessing I receive becomes a bridge for impact.

I declare that I am free to do work I love, on my terms, without fear or limitation.

I am not enslaved by salary; I am empowered by strategy.

My days are filled with fulfillment, my hands create legacy, and my life radiates joy.

I affirm that I walk by faith, not by fear, knowing that God has empowered me to prosper and to leave a legacy. My faith is my fuel. My focus is my force. My FIRE is my freedom.

I decree that I am FIRE'D UP financially independent, purpose-anchored, legacy-minded, and eternally fulfilled.

This is my era of divine acceleration.

This is my season of unstoppable abundance.

This is my testimony of financial freedom, built on wisdom, faith, and favor. Amen.

FINAL CHARGE

The time for hesitation has passed. Freedom is not something that will simply appear one day, it is something you build, step by step, through the choices you make starting now. Everything you need is already within you: the gifts, the vision, and the discipline to create the life you have imagined.

Do not wait for the perfect conditions or permission. The journey to FIRE is not reserved for the lucky or the few but those who decide to be intentional, consistent, and courageous.

You are ready. Take the next step with confidence. Let your vision guide your actions, and let your faith sustain you when the road feels uncertain. You were created to design a life that is abundant in every sense wealthy, grounded in freedom, and on fire with purpose.

Appendices

Appendix A: Case Study Playbooks

In Chapter 4, we explored how to design your Rule of Three Portfolio, the balance of one Active Stream (income you create through your skills), one Passive Stream (systems that scale), and one Compounding Stream (investments that grow).

The following case studies bring those principles to life. Each example shows how real professionals applied the 30-Day Entrepreneur Accelerator Upgrade to test their Rule of Three Portfolio™ in action.

These stories are not new lessons, but proof of concept. They show how the ideas you studied in Chapter 4 look when lived out by everyday professionals across different fields: technology, healthcare, and academia. As you read, use them as a reference point to map out your own 30 or 60-day action plan.

Case Study 1: Daniel: Marketing Manager

Goal: Build first Rule of Three Portfolio™ in 30 Days.

Week 1 – Clarify Your Model (Active Stream):

Daniel chose consulting as his Active Stream: *"I help small businesses increase online sales through targeted Facebook and Instagram ad campaigns."* Focus replaced dabbling. By pitching two local businesses, he secured real conversations.

Week 2 – Set Value-Based Pricing (Active Stream):

Switched from hourly billing ($50/hr) to value pricing. Packaged his service at $1,000/month. Landed his first paying client.

Week 3 – Build Systems, Not Stress (Passive Stream):

Created Google Form for onboarding, checklists for reporting. This freed up time, reduced email clutter, and laid groundwork for scaling into digital assets like a course or membership.

Week 4 – Create a Reinvestment Plan (Compounding Stream):

- 20% into tools.

- 10% into education.

- 70% into Roth IRA index fund.

His first consulting paycheck directly funded long-term wealth.

Result: One new Active Stream, foundation for Passive, and contributions to Compounding.

Case Study 2: Sarah: Registered Nurse

Goal: Diversify income beyond hospital paycheck.

Week 1 – Clarify Your Model (Active Stream):

Pivoted her expertise into tutoring: *"I help nursing students pass their licensing exams through personalized tutoring and test strategies."* By reaching out to schools and online groups, she booked her first session.

Week 2 – Set Value-Based Pricing (Active Stream):

Priced transformation, not hours. Packaged four sessions at $300. Signed up two students for $600 revenue.

Week 3 – Build Systems, Not Stress (Passive Stream):

Streamlined onboarding with a digital form. Compiled notes into a structured study guide—her first Passive digital product.

Week 4 – Create a Reinvestment Plan (Compounding Stream):

● 20% into Zoom Pro.

● 10% into teaching courses.

● 70% into a 403(b)-retirement plan.

Result: Proof she could earn beyond nursing, create a Passive product, and strengthen retirement growth.

Case Study 3: Amit — University Lecturer

Goal: Turn teaching into cash flow.

Week 1 – Clarify Your Model (Active Stream):

Defined his Active Stream: *"I help beginners learn Python through project-based lessons that build real-world apps."* Designed a 4-week outline and announced on LinkedIn.

Week 2 – Set Value-Based Pricing (Active Stream):

Priced a full course at $199 (transformation pricing). Six students enrolled = $1,200 in revenue.

Week 3 – Build Systems, Not Stress (Passive Stream):

Recorded lessons, uploaded to a course platform, automated enrollment, and payment. His teaching became a semi-passive asset.

Week 4 – Create a Reinvestment Plan (Compounding Stream):

- 25% into better video tools.

- 15% into digital ads.

- 60% into index fund brokerage.

Result: Converted teaching into scalable income, built Passive course assets, and seeded compounding wealth.

FIRE'D UP Reflection

Daniel, Sarah, and Amit show the power of The FIRE'd UP Stream Map Framework

- **Active Stream**: Cash flow today.

- **Passive Stream:** Systems that scale.

- **Compounding Stream:** Wealth that grows.

In just 30 days, despite their differing industries, each

proved that financial independence isn't a someday dream. It's a design you can start building today.

Category	Case 1: High Spending, No Strategy (Long Haul)	Case 2: Higher Lifestyle, Smarter Strategy (The Fast Lane)
Annual Income (from paycheck)	$100,000	$100,000
Additional Income (side hustles, rentals, tax savings)	$0	$50,000
Total Effective Income	$100,000	$150,000
Annual Spending (Lifestyle)	$50,000	$55,000 (same lifestyle)
FIRE Number	$1,250,000 (=$50,000 x 25)	$1,250,000 (=$50,000 x 25)
Current Net Worth	$300,000	$300,000
Gap	$950,000	$950,000
Annual Savings	$50,000 (paycheck only)	$120,000 (paycheck + rentals + side income + invested + tax savings)
Years to FIRE	≈ 19 years	≈ 9-10 years

Appendix B: FIRE Pathways in Action

In Chapter 10, we explored how to calculate your FIRE Number and measure your readiness using the four financial pillars.

The following example brings those principles to life. It shows how two professionals with the same paycheck and lifestyle can arrive at financial independence on completely different timelines, depending on how they earn, save, and reinvest.

These case studies are not hypothetical spreadsheets. They illustrate the real-world impact of diversification, disciplined saving, and intentional design.

As you read, consider where your own habits fit and what adjustments could accelerate your timeline to freedom.

Case 1: Single Stream, No Strategy (The Long Road)

Annual Paycheck Income: $100,000

Annual Spending: $50,000

FIRE Number: $50,000 × 25 = $1,250,000

Current Net Worth: $300,000

Gap: $1,250,000 − $300,000 = $950,000

Annual Savings: $50,000 (from one paycheck, no tax optimization, no side hustle reinvestment)

Years to FIRE: $950,000 ÷ $50,000 ≈ 19 years

This professional saves steadily but relies entirely on one paycheck. Without additional income streams, tax strategy, or reinvestment, progress is slow.

At this pace, financial independence is nearly two decades away. The approach is consistent but limited, there is no leverage, only labor.

Case 2: Same Paycheck + Multiple Streams & Smart Strategy (The Fast Lane)

Annual Paycheck Income: $100,000

Additional Side Income & Tax Savings: $50,000

Total Effective Income: $150,000

Annual Spending: $50,000

FIRE Number: $50,000 × 25 = $1,250,000

Current Net Worth: $300,000

Gap: $1,250,000 − $300,000 = $950,000

Annual Savings: $100,000 (primary income + rental property cash flow + side hustle reinvested + tax savings)

Years to FIRE: $950,000 ÷ $100,000 ≈ 9–10 years

These professional uses multiple income streams to increase savings power.

By adding side income, leveraging tax strategies, and reinvesting earnings, they cut their FIRE timeline in half. The same paycheck now produces twice the outcome through smarter structure and stewardship.

FIRE'D UP Insights

Two professionals. Same paycheck. Same lifestyle. Same starting point, but a radically shorter path because the second professional uses tax advantages and multiple streams to accelerate savings, causing them to reach financial independence in half the time. When you combine multiple income streams, disciplined saving, and intentional reinvestment, you accelerate your financial independence.

This is the essence of FIRE readiness: not working harder but designing smarter. The power to shorten your journey is already in your hands.